Praise for *Forming Faith*

This is a book that could change churches and transform families! In *Forming Faith*, Matt, Mike, and Sam present an enormously compelling vision of a new era of church that comes alongside parents, showing them *how* to raise the next generation of passionate, all-in followers of Jesus. In the process, the authors ask challenging questions, urging leaders—and parents—to rethink children's discipleship and to make radical changes as a result. What they envision for our children is no less than what Paul prayed for the people he loved: that they would *experience* the love of Christ in the everyday-ness of real life.

DIANE COMER
Cofounder, Intentional Parents International

Drawing from the Scriptures and significant sociological research on children's and family ministry, Matt, Mike, and Sam make the case that what the next generation needs isn't attractional gimmicks or even programming excellence but biblical orthodoxy, faithful shepherding, and a loving church community. If you're a children's ministry leader, this book will help you move from merely declaring that parents are the primary disciple-makers in kids' lives to intentionally coming alongside parents and growing with them as they learn to shepherd their kids in the faith.

JARED KENNEDY
Editor at The Gospel Coalition and author of *The Beginner's Gospel Story Bible*, *Keeping Your Children's Ministry on Mission*, and *The Story of Martin Luther*

I want our kids to love Jesus, in the seasons of mountaintop victories and heartache-filled valleys. I want it for the ones that live at my house and the ones at yours. *Forming Faith* will open our eyes to what resilient and unwavering faith looks like. Matt, Mike, and Sam are shining a light for us all to follow. May we hold the wisdom they are offering us with much care as we boldly allow faith to be formed in those we minister to. Let this generation be known as a generation that has "on Christ the solid rock I stand" written on their heart, for all of their days.

YANCY
Worship leader, author, and Dove Award winning songwriter/artist

Forming Faith is essential reading for anyone working with children, whether at home or in a church setting. Matt, Mike, and Sam not only highlight our past mistakes but also provide a clear roadmap for correction. Having witnessed their message firsthand, I immediately recognized the necessity of this book. It addresses the pressing needs of today's parents and church leaders, and its wisdom will remain invaluable for generations. Kudos to these authors for their brilliant and masterful work. I wholeheartedly endorse both them and this message!

JIM WIDEMAN
Pastor, author, and pioneer in kidmin and family ministry,
Nashville, TN

If you are in children's ministry, this book will shake up your world. If you are really serious about seeing the next generation follow Jesus, then this book should be on your reading list. This book goes way beyond surface talk and dives deep into how to see kids grow up to love and follow Jesus for a lifetime.

DALE HUDSON
www.buildingchildrensministry.com

forming faith

DISCIPLING THE
NEXT GENERATION IN A
POST-CHRISTIAN CULTURE

MATT MARKINS, MIKE HANDLER,
AND SAM LUCE

MOODY PUBLISHERS
CHICAGO

Edited by Philip F. Newman
Interior design: Puckett Smartt
Cover design and illustration by Spencer Fuller, Faceout Studio
Author photo, Luce: Doe Keh
Author photo, Handler: Monica Winters

ISBN: 978-0-8024-3338-1

Originally delivered by fleets of horse-drawn wagons, the affordable paperbacks from D. L. Moody's publishing house resourced the church and served everyday people. Now, after more than 125 years of publishing and ministry, Moody Publishers' mission remains the same—even if our delivery systems have changed a bit. For more information on other books (and resources) created from a biblical perspective, go to www.moodypublishers.com or write to:

Moody Publishers
820 N. LaSalle Boulevard
Chicago, IL 60610

1 3 5 7 9 10 8 6 4 2

Printed in China

To beloved sons Warren and Hudson,
who are on the path of belonging to God,
believing in Him,
and becoming like Him
by walking in His ways.
Press on in faithfulness.
— Matt Markins

To Sandra, the most beautiful, deserving of every rose.
— Sam Luce

For HandlerHouse, the everyday evidence of God's kindness.

And for Pat and Amy, Swang, Pat and Diane,
Harry, Carri, Mike, Jeremy, Jared, Daryl,
and the others from the church family I grew up in
who helped form my faith.
— Mike Handler

Contents

Introduction

MATT: In the early days of May 2010, the people of the United States were fixated and heartbroken over the images of what's commonly referred to as the BP oil spill. This was a devastating disaster —one from which many are still recovering to this day. This chilling event garnered so much national media attention that, in many ways, it overshadowed another tragic event that took place in the days following.

The event I'm referring to is the Nashville flood. Are you familiar? I have a particular interest in this flood, because it brought with it almost three feet of water running through the entire first floor of our two-story house.

On May 1 and 2, 2010, seventeen inches of rain fell in Middle Tennessee. This was the highest two-day rainfall in the area going back 140 years. The reservoir system, including Old Hickory and Percy Priest Lakes, continued to collect water until they were about to burst. On the afternoon of Sunday, May 2, both lakes opened their dams within minutes of each other, sending a wall of water rushing into the Cumberland River channel, which spilled her banks, and flood waters assumed temporary residence in our quiet little neighborhood at the bend in the river.

Katie (my wife) and the boys were frantically moving our possessions to the second floor of our house. Katie was lugging framed family pictures and generational heirlooms as the boys were carrying totes of LEGO bricks and favorite worn books to a dry place of rescue. "Would this even be high enough?" they wondered. Would the flood waters reach the second floor? We didn't know. No one knew.

As Katie put the final items on the second floor, she threw the master switch at the junction box to shut down the power supply to the entire house. As she closed the front door behind her, she stepped down into our front lawn, which now held three feet of water that was rapidly approaching the top step of our front porch.

Our little one-way-in-one-way-out neighborhood street was already sitting under several feet of water at that point. By the time it had occurred to anyone that evacuating would be necessary, it was too late. This was a situation where there was no master plan. No protocol. There was no team captain. There wasn't even information coming from the local authorities. Our little neighborhood was "on our own." So in typical Tennessee fashion, neighborhood escape came in the form of—a bass boat.

And like any good husband, I was . . .

Out of town. I missed the whole thing.

Friends, you have no idea how painful it was for me to miss this entire ordeal. Not only to be there for my family, but selfishly speaking, I love a good crisis. I'm an adrenaline junkie, and for me this would have been better than Disney World.

By the time I flew into town, it was that evening. Katie and I embraced as she cried, telling me each vivid detail of the day in HD-like clarity. It all seemed so astounding. So "other." Difficult to wrap my head around.

I just had to see it for myself. It was killing me.

The following day was one of those 100 percent sunshine, blue-sky kind of days, which felt strangely odd in light of the previous day's circumstances. I rode out to our house via boat. We docked on our front porch, pushed open the door, and waded through our house in waist-deep water. Talk about an eerie feeling—to see your remaining possessions just . . . floating. I can still see the dining room table s-l-o-w-l-y swirling in the middle of the room, hovering on the thick, brown, muddy Cumberland River water. The juxtaposition of the flowers resting perfectly still in the vase on the table, in light of their newly arranged environment, was jolting.

It was such an odd experience. Yet, my FOMO (fear of missing out) had been temporarily satisfied. I may have missed the day of action, but at least I was able to put my eyes on the damage.

I was dropped off at a neighbor's house to make room for others who needed boating transportation. The house where I was standing was the only one on the street that was built high enough that the river did not breach the threshold of the first floor. So I'm left there . . . by myself. . . . Big mistake.

As a person of action, it didn't sit well with me as I watched various neighbors' possessions just float slowly down the street. Which was actually not a street at that point—it was a river. I began to think, *You know, I bet I can make it back to the house. Come to think of it, there are a couple of things I'd like to go back and check on. It's only three houses away . . .*

I began to make my way down the porch steps . . . into the water. By the time I waded to the street the river current was chest high. With the sun beaming down and reflecting off the water, I began to work my way down the street. With each step, the fear, isolation, and anxiety increased exponentially.

That was the moment when reality sank in. As I walked against the current in chest-high water, my average-developed frontal lobe in my thirty-four-year-old male brain began to think, *Matt, you are no longer walking on your street. You are walking IN THE RIVER! And, you are walking upstream against the current!*

How is it possible that I could be walking in a spot that I've walked hundreds of times before, yet I did not recognize where I was? I built that house. I cleared that property by myself with a D5 bulldozer. I knew this neighborhood like the back of my hand—the gentle curve in the road, where to step and not to step, the oldest trees, paths carved in the woods, and the custom features of each house. And yet, at that moment, I didn't recognize where I was anymore.

I felt isolated. Fearful. And, I was walking against the current.

Does this sound familiar? In so many ways, if you are in ministry, you are walking the same terrain you've been walking for quite some time. Same church. Same community of kids and families. You should be able to recognize your environment, so why does nothing seem familiar? We are now walking in a flood of new circumstances. And against an aggressive current of persistent cultural change. You may be standing in the same spot, so this should feel normal. Yet it doesn't. This is what we are experiencing today as we aim to form the faith of children.

It's our job to prepare them. It's our job to participate with God in forming their faith.

So, what do we do with this unique moment in which we find ourselves? Much like how I couldn't just "wish" the floodwaters away so that everything could go back to normal, we can't simply long for the nostalgia of simpler times. The world in which we live today is filled with new complexities, and our children will inherit a future world few of us can imagine and many of us will not live to see. And it's our job to prepare them. It's our job to participate with God in forming their faith.

Sam, Mike, and I have written *Forming Faith* to help you do just that—to disciple the next generation in a post-Christian culture.

As we journey forward together, you will notice that *Forming Faith* is a book about *perspective*. Our aim is to give you a window of insight—a healthy, research-backed, and biblical perspective—to disciple today's kids fruitfully in a world flooded with complexity.

You will also notice that this book has two parts: Part 1 (chapters 1–4) and Part 2 (chapters 5–8). Think of these two parts as the two sashes to one window.

Part 1: In the first window of perspective you will be challenged to analyze and evaluate the way we do ministry today, followed by a clear plan (map) that you can implement immediately. The map of children's ministry that we use today—where did it come from? Was it designed for today or was it blueprinted for a bygone era? And what *should* it be? Of all of the things we could be doing to effectively and biblically reach and disciple children, what should receive our focus, time, attention, and resources? In chapters 1–4, we lay out a clear map to lead us forward to reach and disciple kids in today's context based on the ancient, unmovable faithfulness of Christian orthodoxy combined with fresh research that takes into account the nuanced complexities of today's world. The solutions provided in Part 1 will give you the clear objectives you need to disciple children fruitfully in a post-Christian context.

Part 2: The second window of perspective addresses the elephant in the room: *parents*. It's common in today's church to hear things like, "Parents are the primary spiritual influence over their kids," "We must equip parents," and even, "Our church partners with parents." But how are we doing in these endeavors? Most churches want desperately to see parents discipling their own children, but report that it's simply not happening in most homes. We've conducted groundbreaking research that will give you fresh insight and provide you a purposeful plan to engage parents most effectively to form the faith of the next generation.

In addition, we've designed each chapter with a "Gaining Perspective" exercise to help you maximize the insight in the book, either by yourself or with your team. Our desire with these few questions before you read the chapter is to challenge your assumptions and foster creative thinking to faithfully apply the truths you find in the chapter that follows. With a flood of cultural landscape changes, no matter how familiar we are with the surroundings, we benefit from intentional navigation points, and we've designed tools and a process to help you lead in today's world.

Sam, Mike, and I are honored to take a journey with you. We've prayed for this book and its readers that there might be eternal impact for generations to come. May the words, ideas, and concepts we share in the pages ahead be a blessing and add value to the hard work you're already engaged in. For the children of today, and the church of tomorrow, let's form lasting faith in the children in our churches and communities.

So that you may become blameless and pure, "children of God
without fault in a warped and crooked generation."
Then you will shine among them like stars in the sky
as you hold firmly to the word of life.
PHILIPPIANS 2:15–16A (NIV)

Gaining Perspective

As Matt mentioned, prior to each chapter we want to provide an opportunity to gain perspective about where you, the reader, might be as it relates to the information you'll engage with throughout the following pages. These will mostly take the form of experiences or questions. Our purpose in providing these is simply to help make this book a meaningful experience.

- On a piece of paper, draw a horizontal line and on the left write the word "church." On the right, write the word "home." Where on this line would you place the burden of discipleship of children within your church? Plot that point before you begin reading this chapter.

- Write down why you plotted the point where you did.

- What were the factors in your own discipleship that informed this decision? Include experiences, people, and entities that made a lasting impact.

• • •

We're Using Old Maps

---◇---

A healthy perspective can change everything.

MATT: A few years ago, my son wanted to go on a Caribbean cruise for his senior trip. I'm not really into the cruise ship scene, but this is how our eldest wanted to commemorate the completion of his journey through high school. So we started planning, saving, and replanning. It was one of those 2020, 2021, 2022 cruise trips that kept getting delayed year after year due to COVID-19.

The day finally arrived. We pushed off, pointed southward as the evening sunlight was fading, and we set sail hoping for a grand adventure like no other. After a day of excursions together in our first port, we returned to our seaworthy vessel. We cleaned up and were just about to head to one of the restaurants on board when we noticed that the ship was beginning to move. Katie, my wife, remarked something like, "Guys, we're moving—come out to the balcony!"

As we stepped out onto the deck we noticed hundreds of other families participating in this ritual of waving goodbye to the locals as we began sailing away. I remember thinking at this moment how satisfied I felt about the day (though I don't particularly like cruises), and I was even looking forward to the new adventures that awaited our family in the days to come. Then, suddenly I was jolted from these thoughts with a grinding sound as the entire ship seemed to sway just the slightest little bit. *Did I just feel what I think I felt?* I wondered. *Have we stopped?* Confusion ensued among the ship's passengers as we hypothesized and theorized from our balconies— passing observations from left to right through buzzing chatter. This situation seemed . . . odd. What could it be?

Our cruise ship was stuck on a sandbar.[1]

When your vacation makes international news, it ceases to be a vacation. Due to minor damage on the ship's hull, we were unable to continue sailing. The following day the captain announced that this cruise was officially canceled, and there would be more communication in the days to come. With a ship that accommodates four thousand people, this was going to take a while.

It's remarkable how quickly your mindset shifts from "What fun things are we going to do today?" to "How are we going to get off of this boat? And how in the world are they going to get a few thousand people home?!" It's a swift change in perspective.

Yet, over the course of the next few days I was struck by the incongruence of the cruise liner's perspective on communication in light of the very real circumstances. Where passengers were thirsty for communication on basic disembarking logistics, the cruise liner persisted with printing and distributing the daily newsletter promoting festive family events, karaoke locations, theme nights, and the adjusted times of the dinner show. Even the cruise director (you know, the overly hyper-energetic guy who pops onto the loudspeaker every ninety minutes to share the latest exciting announcement) went about his job as if it were business as usual. Actual information about the disembarking of the ship dripped out at a very slow pace, and passengers were forced to discover most critical information on their own by waiting in very long customer service lines.

The cruise liner needed to drop the daily-fun script, and to move to a new script—one that matched the moment. By not doing this, chaos and anxiety ensued. The cruise leaders lacked perspective on how to navigate the moment they were facing.

When I think about our encounter of being stuck on a sandbar, I can't help but think about the cultural moment the church is facing. Sam, Mike, and I—all three of us—deeply love the church and have dedicated our lives to the strengthening of the body of Christ.

We stand beside you as ministers of the gospel and we ask, Do we have a healthy perspective on how to form the faith of today's kids? Gaining perspective on forming faith—that's what this book is all about.

Forming Childhood Faith in Today's New World

I'm an imaginative person. Will you join me for a moment? Let's tap into our imaginations and think of the face of a child or a young person whom you care deeply about. Perhaps it's your son, daughter, or grandchild, a child or student in your ministry, a relative, or a student at your school. Now, when you think of the future world they are headed into, do you have concern about how this world will form children? Does your heart leap forward with a longing to somehow ensure their faith is formed to be resiliently rooted in Christ?

Pastor Jon Tyson has said, "Secularism is here and it's coming and we're probably in a moment in our generation of such decline, we probably won't be able to stop it."[2] Today's eight-year-old child (the age of a young person at the heart of your church's children's

Does your heart leap forward with a longing to somehow ensure their faith is formed to be resiliently rooted in Christ?

ministry) will spend his or her adult life primarily between the years 2032–2092. As time ticks onward, these children will likely grow into young adults and experience the expansion of secularism through items that are new to us like artificial intelligence (AI), the metaverse, transgenderism, emerging digital currencies, ChatGPT, transhumanism, non-fungible token currencies (NFTs), and a long list of other seemingly Orwellian ideas.

In light of the current secular trajectory, it's fair to ask, "Is the church adequately preparing today's eight-year-old to thrive in his or her faith in a very different, post-Christian, highly secularized future?"

After a decade of commissioning eleven research projects and ministry impact studies, this prevailing thought has become abundantly clear to Sam, Mike, and me: *we're using old maps.*

Acknowledging the Map Is Outdated

I've always been fascinated with maps. I can remember gazing at ancient maps in elementary school textbooks. For our eldest son's fifth birthday party, Katie and I made fake "old" pirate maps as invitations, where we crumpled the paper and burnt the edges to make them look officially aged (so fun!). And any time I come across an old regional US map, I'm always squinting to find my hometown.

One thing I've noticed is that one's view on mapping technology is largely dependent on your generational upbringing. My baby boomer parents used the ole Rand McNally maps. Remember those? They were so ridiculously massive that when my mom would open the map up in the front seat of the minivan, my stepdad would have to crane his neck around the obstruction to have a clear view out the front windshield so he didn't run off the road!

Then, by 1989, if your family was on the leading edge, the Garmin may have found its way into your vacation vehicle of choice. Thanks to NASA, the space age ported right to our dashboard, and we would follow the green line to our final destination.

Then in 1997, along came MapQuest. As a Gen Xer, I started ministry in a role that required quite a bit of travel about this time and thought MapQuest was brilliant. What made it so smart was that if I were leaving Nashville, Tennessee, headed to Knoxville, then driving over to Charlotte, North Carolina, and from there to Atlanta, then to Birmingham, Alabama, and finally back to Nashville, I'd print out each leg of the trip and give it its own manilla folder, and off I'd go. I practically needed a filing cabinet in the back seat!

Then for our younger millennial and Gen Z brothers and sisters, of course you remember the convenience of Apple Maps when it launched in 2012 (not to mention Google Maps and Waze!) right there in the palm of your hand. We've come a long way in terms of mapping technology, and we tend to tap the push notification when that software update is available, as we always want the most updated information.

Recently I came across another kind of map just outside San Antonio, Texas, as we toured the old Spanish, Catholic missions (ending with the Alamo). While touring Mission San Jose, we entered an adobe-clad room, and there it was, stretched across the wall about five feet tall by about eight feet wide. I stopped dead in my tracks while Katie and the boys moved on to the next room. Check it out.[3]

Have you ever had an experience where you sense that an object is speaking to you? Like a line from a song, a verse from the Bible, a scene from a movie, or even the sight of a famous painting? I was

having one of those moments. I couldn't move. Katie and the boys had to come back and get me. There's a powerful story here.

This map was published in the 1500s. Created by the Italians, it was, no doubt, a well-funded endeavor to accomplish such a great feat. With limited visibility, limited mobility, and limited technology (compared to today, of course), look at what they created! It's quite remarkable. So, let's use our imaginations once more and pretend we could bring these Italian mapmakers back from the dead and have them right in our presence.

What would we say to them?

I think we would say something like, "Wow. Thank you. Thank you for the price you paid and what you created with such limited information and technology compared to what we have today. Again, thank you. That is impressive work." That's gratitude. We would lead with abundant gratitude for such an outstanding achievement.

I think what we would *not* say is, "You guys are a bunch of idiots. Look at how off you were compared to satellite maps." No, we would never say that! We would lead with a spirit of gratitude for all they accomplished with limited technology and mobility in a bygone era.

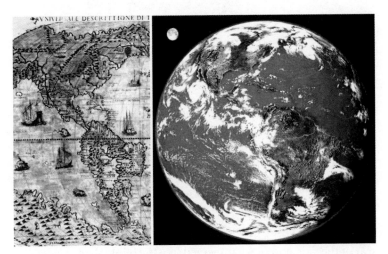

But here's the thing. If today's child educators were still using *this* old map to teach geography, geopolitical boundaries, and navigation to our children, we'd be outraged! We'd say, "This is an outdated map. We have more information now than we did when this map was created. If we keep using this old map to educate our children, it's going to lead to long-term consequences."

Church leaders and Christ-following parents, this is where we are in the church today: *children's ministry today is using old maps.*

When it comes to children's ministry, we simply have more information today than when our current map was drafted. We have more information about:

- The use of edutainment
- The importance of Bible literacy and Scripture engagement
- Mental health and adverse childhood experiences
- Mobile technology, social media, and digital disruption
- The influence of loving, caring adult volunteers who engage children relationally

- The frantic pace of the family (travel e.g., sports)
- And not to mention the primary factors that lead to lasting faith in children

Where Did the Current Model of Children's Ministry Come From?

I distinctly remember a cross-country family vacation from my childhood when we departed Denver driving east. I can still recall looking out the back window of the minivan and seeing the Rocky Mountains off in the distance. I fell asleep that evening in the back seat of the van, and in what seemed like the blink of an eye, I woke up and asked my stepdad, "Where are we?" He responded, "Oh, we're just a couple of hours away from St. Louis." (He had driven all through the night.) "What?!" I exclaimed. "How did we get here?!"

For the one sleeping in the back of the minivan, you really don't know exactly how you arrived at another city almost twelve hours away. Although I was "there" in the minivan, I wasn't actually experiencing the navigational process from Denver to St. Louis the way my stepdad was. I was there . . . but I wasn't there.

For many of us working, leading, or volunteering in children's ministry, it's kind of the same. We are working off of a map that was drafted decades ago. We (Boomers and Xers) may have been around then, but most of us weren't the ones who drafted it. We were there, but not there. Then for our younger millennial and Gen Z brothers and sisters, the old map of children's ministry may be all you've ever known. You were likely raised on the old map.

Let's pause for a moment to reflect on where exactly today's common model of children's ministry comes from. Most children's ministries today were built off 1980s and 1990s assumptions that were published in books and blogs and taught at workshops in the early 2000s; and most of us are still operating off of this common blueprint today. We even call our contemporary model of children's ministry "innovative" because it uses current entertainment, screens, videos, mobile technology, and discussion-based child development pedagogy. Although today's children's ministry is oftentimes referred to as innovative, the reality is that it's a blueprint designed for the past. Like when we compare satellite maps to our Italian mapmakers from the 1500s, we simply have more information now than we did when today's model was designed. And recent outcomes research data says it's not working.

Gen Zers (those born between 1997 and 2012) are the product of the old map of children's ministry, and the eldest among them are launching into the world as young adults as of the time of the writing of this chapter. As David Kinnaman, a leading Christian researcher and president of Barna Group, has said, "The Church is woefully unprepared for Gen Z."[4] Meaning, we had the chance to form them as children, then as students. But only 10 percent of them—whom Kinnaman calls "resilient disciples"[5]—are thriving in their faith as young adults, still engaged in the church.

> We need a new map that's *known* to form lasting faith in kids.

A 10 percent success rate is a hard pill for all of us to swallow. To make this practical, as a leader of an organization myself, I think, *If our ministry was losing 90 percent of our church partners or donors, how long would we be able to remain in ministry?* Not long. We would have to come to grips with the fact that our approach to success was failing.

As faithful pastors, leaders, and shepherds, we are wrestling with both our outcome rate of only "10 percent" success and the inadequate process described as "woefully unprepared" by David Kinnaman.

Our approach to forming faith isn't working. Why? *Children's ministry today is using old maps that were built for an era gone by.*

At best, the rate at which we are forming thriving disciples is low. We need a new map. We need a map that's *known* to form lasting faith in kids. This will require courageous pastors and parents like you who are willing to learn new (and old) insights to draft a map that's both rooted in ancient, biblical faithfulness and updated to address the complexities that surround today's child.

The Power of Perspective

Maps are wonderful navigation tools because they provide perspective to users. A good map allows them to know where they are and how to navigate where they're headed, but it also provides the perspective of the trip's scale, direction, and distance, and what might be around them along the way. While a GPS is useful for turn-by-turn directions, a map is beneficial in navigation and discovery. This is the power of perspective: it changes our journey because it orients us to where we are in the context of what's around us.

Likewise, windows allow a means to view, know, and understand the world around us. The windows on the cover of this book represent God's two agents of formation: church and home. These two entities benefit from the windows on their walls, which help them to understand the atmosphere of the outside world as well as provide light and warmth to those inside the walls. Windows, like maps, provide an opportunity for perspective.

As we move forward together through this book, like looking through a window, we must first grapple with the perspective we're choosing as we consider ministry to children. Understanding the point of view you're starting this journey with will help you gain the proper perspective as we think carefully about the why, what, who, how, and where faith is formed. As we move into chapter 2, we will grapple with two very different perspectives on not only how to engage children, but how to shape the future of the world. Consider these two perspectives as we prepare to press onward:

One: If our primary investment in children—the most vulnerable among us—is in *shielding* and *entertaining* them, we will likely form within them a safe-yet-fragile foundation..

Two: However, if our primary investment in the most vulnerable among us is in *forming* them, we will become artisans who shape a generation whose inner spiritual resilience is so compelling that future communities will gasp at their Christlike beauty.

A healthy perspective can change everything. May we find the hope, courage, conviction, and compassion we need as we evaluate our perspective on effectively forming the faith of the next generation.

QUESTIONS FOR REFLECTION

1. Would you say of your church's children's ministry, "We are adequately preparing the kids to thrive in their faith in a highly secularized future that may be far different from today's"?

2. What makes your children's ministry successful? How do/would we know that?

3. Is there a gap between the vision, mission, strategy, and goals of your children's ministry . . . compared to how you actually operate?

4. What are the primary methodologies, programs, and tactics you are relying on to achieve your goals, mission, and vision? What do you spend the most amount of time, energy, and resources on?

Gaining Perspective

- What is the most recent addition you made to your ministry *environment*? What were the costs of that change (financial, relational, logistical, etc.)?

- What is the most recent change you made to your ministry *practices*? What were the costs of that change (financial, relational, logistical, etc.)?

- What's the next big change you hope to make in your ministry, and why?

. . .

CHAPTER TWO

A Little Less Disney,
a Bit More Mister Rogers

—✦—

*"Childhood lies at the very heart of who we are
and who we become."*[1]—FRED ROGERS

SAM: Ours is a distracted age. The past fifty years have been a relentless pursuit of *new* at the expense of the things that matter most. We like to hear positive stories of innovation and cutting-edge ideas that entertain and *wow*. We live in a culture that Neil Postman says has an "infinite appetite for distractions."[2] Our world has been so affected by the Darwinian idea that all progress is good and that every iteration is better than what was before. We have created this insatiable appetite for *new* and *next* that seems to be consuming our culture. Sherry Turkle says that our march of technological progress and chasing what is new has consequences: we miss things. "It seems nearly impossible to have an uninterrupted conversation at a family dinner," she writes. "We catch ourselves not looking into the eyes of our children or taking the time to talk with them just to have a few more hits of our email."[3] Places that have been sacred spaces for child discipleship are routinely interrupted by our devices and screens that promise so much and deliver so little.

Not only are adults more distracted now, but our kids are more distracted than ever before. We have allowed the passions of innovation, creativity, and entertainment—divorced from a personal presence and intentional relationships—to drive the programming in our churches. As a result, we are more alone than ever; Sherry Turkle calls it "Alone Together."[4] *We long for transformation, yet settle for entertainment.* We trade transcendence for information. Yet the more we chase knowledge and experiences, the less we experience what it is like to be known. We crave distraction when what we need is transformation.

Two Kingdoms, Two Very Different Perspectives

One of my heroes was a man who understood life, children, and the power of forgiveness and redemption, known to his family and friends as Fred—known to millions of devoted fans as Mister Rogers. I got to know him later in life. I didn't grow up watching Mister Rogers because when I was a child, we didn't have a TV, the internet wasn't invented yet, and cassette tapes were considered cutting-edge. My early days did not include an endless parade of entertainment. Instead, they were filled with wonder and punctuated by silence.

My siblings and I would spend several weeks on my grandparents' dairy farm each summer. We filled our days with discoveries, climbing trees, and chasing wild cats. I remember watching *Mister Rogers' Neighborhood* for the first time at my grandparents' house because they had a TV. When you grow up without one, every television set you see is fascinating. There was something about Mister Rogers that was so captivating. I wouldn't fully understand why this was true till I got older. I remember spending those summer afternoons watching someone I would grow to love, respect, and hope to be like someday.

My grandmother worked at a nursing home in eastern North Dakota, and she would often bring us with her to work. The residents were kind enough to allow my sister and me to watch what we wanted to on the lone TV located in the rec room. Most days, we watched *Mister Rogers' Neighborhood* and *The Muppet Show*. I wasn't a daily Rogers viewer, but the times I watched made an impression that has grown in its influence over the years.

Mister Rogers, an ordained Presbyterian minister, had a way about him. He talked to kids like they were people. He talked about hard things. He stepped into the difficult and did not distract kids from sorrow; instead, he discipled them through it. Mister Rogers understood children. He understood their value and what should form them. His words influenced the collective imagination of an entire generation. Yet he was more than an entertainer; he was a prophet. What he said in his time is even more true of our time. He didn't see distraction as anything positive for adults, and especially not for children. He famously said, "Our society is much more interested in information than wonder, in noise rather than silence."[5] Our world over the past half-century has been filled with information and noise. Our job as disciplers of children is to fight through the clutter, incite wonder, and promote careful reflection of the things in life that matter most.

The global pandemic of 2020 did to kids' ministry what it did to everything else in our world. It forced us to stop and ask, "Why are we doing what we are doing? Are we doing the things that matter most?"

The answer for some items was yes, but for many things, being forced to stop the cycle of events and weekend services as we had always done them made us realize something needed to change.

When I slowed down and tried to make sense of a situation that caused countless kids to encounter worry, sorrow, and pain, my mind drifted toward Fred.

Kids' pastors often face pressure from parents, church leaders, or themselves—and sometimes it's all three. This pressure, which is sometimes spoken but generally unspoken, is for our ministries to be more like Disney. We feel pressure to get results in a world that has radically changed. Matt, in chapter 1, clearly articulated that the typography of the ministry landscape has changed. We can't keep doing ministry in the new world we find ourselves in with old maps. We have to allow these pressures we feel to force us to ask better questions and find better solutions.

I have often looked at how Disney engages kids as inspiration for engaging the kids I lead. I have also had people kindly suggest that we take a look at how Disney does things. I even went to Disney and have sent staff members to Disney for inspiration for ministry. And I'm not the only one to have done this. This was a movement within children's ministry—and still is. We thought, *If we can only make our ministry spaces and experiences more like Disney, we can engage children more effectively and lead them to love and follow Jesus.*

The two kingdoms Walt and Fred built resulted from two visions of the world.

However, the older I get and the longer I do kids' ministry, the more I realize that Walt Disney's idea of child formation was wrong, and Fred Rogers' was right. (To be clear, I am not a Disney hater; I have taken the required pilgrimage to Orlando with my family.)

When you look at the aesthetics of the two kingdoms both Walt and Fred built, they reflect how each saw the world. Walt's world is a perfect version of what our world should look like. His kingdom includes shiny songs playing everywhere. Every restaurant serves chicken strips and hotdogs. There's never any dust, not a sliver of chipped paint. Excellence and creativity abound. Fred's world, on the other hand, was simple, even plain. His puppets showed wear, and his set grew old along with him. Two worlds trying to reach the same kids.

The two kingdoms they built resulted from two visions of the world. Walt created a world that is an escape from the real world. Fred lived in a neighborhood and showed kids how to navigate the real world.

I Think We Are Going to Have to Start Over

When Fred Rogers gave the commencement address to the Marquette University graduates of 2001, he did something for each of those in attendance; he gave them the gift of silence. A silence that was filled with purpose. He said:

> Anyone who has ever graduated from a university, anyone who has ever been able to sustain a good work has had at least one person—and often many—who believed in him or her. We just don't get to be competent human beings without many different investments from others. I'd like to give you all an invisible gift: a gift of silence to think about those who nourish you at the deepest part of your being—anyone who has ever loved you and wanted what was best for you in life. Some of those people may be right here today. Some may be far away; some may even be in heaven. But if they've encouraged you to come closer to what you know to be essential about life, I'd like you to have a silent minute to think of them.[6]

Those sixty seconds were quietly powerful. I encourage you to receive that same gift right where you are today: Put down this book, set a timer for one minute, and sit in silence, reflecting on that person or persons who invested in you and allowed you to become who you are today.

Fred went on in his speech to say that whomever you have been thinking about would be so thankful you thought of them with such gratitude.

He concluded by saying, "You don't ever have to do anything sensational in order to love or to be loved. The real drama of life—that which matters most—is rarely center stage or in the spotlight."[7]

Discipleship, particularly the discipleship of children, is rarely center stage or in the spotlight. However, when we are alone with ourselves for one minute, the person we remember most is not who entertained us; it is the person who showed up in our lives—the one who discipled us.

Until 2020, in the history of the world, the church had not been kept from physically meeting together. The year 2020 was one of the more challenging in recent memory. I talked to an elderly member of our community who was in his nineties, and he said not being able to meet was the most difficult thing he has ever faced. From someone who has lived in our world for ninety-plus years, that is saying something.

So, my question is this: Is it possible COVID-19 brought us hidden blessings that we missed because we so badly wanted to get back to "normal"? What if God allowed COVID to get the church to start over? Because I think we are going to have to.

The early church obeyed the Great Commission (Matt. 28:16–20) because persecution was the impetus. The Roman roads, built by the Roman Empire, were the conduit for the Great Commission to be fulfilled in their time. What if COVID was a way for us to realize we can't do church the same as we have been doing it? Maybe we *shouldn't* be doing church the way we have been doing it.

Something needs to change, but what, exactly? If we are to steward this cultural moment well, here is what needs to be different.

Reset #1: Who Matters More than What

Who your kids are becoming matters more than what your children's ministry spaces look like. Discipleship needs more thought and investment than environments do. There has been much focus on excellence in kids and youth environments and not enough on how we create lifelong followers of Christ. What things do we need to teach, and how can we teach those things to kids in a way that creates lasting faith in Jesus? These are the primary questions that need to consume our thoughts and drive our budgets; things like spaces and environments are then designed out of that vision for child discipleship.

Reset #2: Real Transcends Virtual

We need to train a community of people who can teach the Scriptures and transmit their faith to the next generation. Plug-and-play Bible stories are excellent and professional, yet often at the expense of being tangible and authentic. Kids need more than just information; they need incarnation. Our small group leaders need to better know the families they serve. Then, if we are unable to meet in person again, they have a human connection point between the church and the home. During the height of the pandemic at our church, we leveraged video and technology to hold events on Zoom and started our own YouTube channel. What made more of an impact wasn't those things, as great as they were. It was letters in the mail and dropping stuff off on porches. Eye-to-eye human encounters are ancient, time-tested, authentic, and classic. In an isolated world starving for relational intimacy, it's the real that transcends what's virtual and cool.

Reset #3: Small Is the New Big

Our church is large. Now, I'm not picking on large churches, but the return rate of kids at our large campuses as we started to come back from COVID was around 10 percent, way below expectations. At our smaller campuses, the return rate was 80 percent. One year after coming back to in-person meetings, our larger campuses are still only at 75 percent, while our smaller campuses are back to 100 percent. What is the difference? Community, accountability, relationship; in a word, it's discipleship. In our smaller locations, discipleship is visceral. In our larger campus, discipleship is optional. This has to change. Churches of all sizes and scales need to make "small" a part of their discipleship culture. And to my megachurch friends, ask those at smaller churches how to do this better. We can all learn from each other.

How Were Walt and Fred So Different?

A concern for who our kids are becoming, showing up in tangible ways, and recognizing that small things matter made Fred Rogers a household name and a national hero. For decades, kids' ministries have modeled themselves after Walt Disney rather than Fred Rogers. We must move from these old maps of edutainment. If we use this moment to build new maps for ministry, our kids' ministries will look more like Mister Rogers and less like Disney.

Walt Built a Fantasy World, Fred Lived in a Neighborhood

There is nothing wrong with fantasy. Kids need fairy stories. J. R. R. Tolkien and C. S. Lewis were both shaped by fairy stories; however, they had different takes on the ontological value of stories. Tolkien believed fairy stories were reflective of God, that they were an example of sub-creation. Lewis thought you could smuggle truth into fairy stories and steal past the watchful dragons that would not give faith a hearing. In this debate, I side more with Lewis. Fairy tales are more valuable in helping us escape this world—not for the escape alone, but to show us what is broken and how to fix it. Fairy stories should not be only an escape; they should contain truth that entertains our minds and changes our hearts.

Walt's world, on the whole, is an escape from reality, sustained by entertainment. You enter the park, and you enter the world as it should be—no trash on the ground, no gum on the sidewalk, and no tears in any eye. It's perfect. It plays to our right desire for a better world. It reminds us in miniature form that our world—the real world—is a shadow, and our hearts long for a perfect world free of sin and pain.

Fred's world had fantasy elements in it. But Fred never lied. He said we were going to the land of make-believe. His fiction was grounded in reality and founded in faith. Fred lived in a neighborhood like you and me. Although his set was old and his puppets were tired, he connected with kids in a way few others have. Mister Rogers had friends come by who struggled with difficult issues like divorce, physical disability, and even race. He didn't create an alternate universe by which he could escape reality. He lived in a house and told kids when make-believe was happening. He used fairy stories to smuggle truth.

Walt Entertained Kids, Fred Empowered Kids

Walt's world is all about connecting kids to fun in order to entertain them. This is a trap I fell into early in my career in children's ministry. For years I would ask kids at the end of the service if they'd had fun. I wanted the church to be an escape for them from the difficulties of home and school. The problem with entertaining kids is that you have to out-create yourself every week. Kids go to Disney one or two times a year, max. They come to church one to three times a month on average. Entertainment may bring them, but we don't have the budget, creativity, or time to create programs that rival or compete with Disney's magic.

Fred's "Home" Was a House, Walt's a Castle

Mister Rogers didn't distract kids from the pain and questions that were making them sad or scared. He looked into the camera and spoke from his heart to theirs. He did this because he remembered what it was like to be a child.

He wasn't trying to force kids to grow up and act older than they were. He was interested in helping them understand that we grow, learn, and love in families, communities, and neighborhoods. It isn't castles and clouds that make us forget our problems for a day. It's the embodiment of being in a particular time and a particular place. Discipleship requires that we ask different questions. I stopped asking the kids in our church, "Did you have fun?" I now ask, "What did you learn about God today?" "How did you see Jesus in the story today?" Last, "How did the Holy Spirit show up in a special way?"

Children don't need to be entertained as much as they need to be loved and listened to. Anyone can play a video. Anyone can create an event that is nonstop excitement. The church has gotten really good at production values and excellence. Where our excellence shines brightest is in creating fun places for our kids. We are going to talk more about that in the next chapter. Being fun is not a bad thing as long as fun is not our primary goal and not the way we judge our effectiveness in ministry. We have fun down. What we need to get better at is remembering we were kids once, telling kids the truth, and listening to kids and looking at them in the face when they are speaking to us. Kids like going to Disney, but they live in neighborhoods.

Walt Was More Concerned about Your Experience, Fred with Who You Are Becoming

Walt was focused on how his park made you feel. He paid close attention to sights, sounds, and smells. Fred was more concerned with who you are becoming. In his now-famous interview with Mister Rogers in *Esquire* magazine, Tom Junod wrote, "There was an energy to him, however, a fearlessness, an unashamed insistence on intimacy."[8] This is the problem with entertainment: it leads to a consumer-driven faith where we show up and get our money's worth. The production values are high, and we expect nothing less. Excellence matters, we assert.[9] God is a God of creativity and excellence, we tell ourselves. Yet when God sent His Son into the world, He did so in such an ordinary way. He sent Jesus in such a way that most people failed to recognize Him because they were looking for a conquering king, not a helpless baby.

Fred's idea was different. He was not driven by flash, but by substance. He was not about entertainment. He was about incarnation—an insistence on intimacy. He showed us that loving your neighbor well matters. We must be more obsessed with *who our kids are becoming*, not just how we can *get more kids* coming. If we shift more toward who our kids are becoming, we will lead differently and love differently; we'll focus on things that

> We have to build communities where discipleship is a priority, where showing up is a reflex, where we speak the truth and embody it.

don't just take their minds off their pain, but instead point to the one who can destroy their pain with the power of His love. We have to build communities where discipleship is a priority, where showing up is a reflex, where we speak the truth and embody it.

I have served in the same church for twenty-seven years. I asked our current youth pastor, who was three years old when I arrived, what he remembers most about our kids' ministry—what messages or stories stood out to him. He said, "Actually, I forgot pretty much everything you taught us when we were kids." (Not something you want to put on your résumé.) "But," he continued, "what I do remember was when I was in the hospital, and you came to pray with me before I had surgery and gave me a video game and told me I was going to be okay, that God was with me." This isn't a story about me and some brilliant discipleship scheme I created. I just remembered what it was like to be a kid and be scared of hospitals, and I showed up. It's the small things that matter more than we realize.

How Can Children's Ministry Become More Like Mister Rogers and Less Like Disney?

As people of the Word, we know Jesus was the ultimate *relational* disciple maker. He engaged the woman at the well with tremendous empathy. He taught His disciples everything they would need to lead and grow His church. He brought transformational spiritual insight to the masses on a hillside. He was known to attend festivals, meals, parties, synagogue assemblies, and weddings. He even said, "Let the little children come to me, and do not hinder them, for the kingdom of heaven belongs to such as these" (Matt. 19:14 NIV).

When it comes to discipling children, Jesus is our ultimate model. That is why we find this Walt Disney vs. Fred Rogers framework so incredibly helpful. It challenges us to reflect and evaluate what Matt was talking about in chapter 1 regarding the old map of children's ministry. In our right desire to lead well, have we focused on the wrong things? Should the "Disney mentality" be the prevailing thinking as we move into our increasingly post-Christian culture?

What we can learn from Mister Rogers will lead children's

ministry into a brighter future, one that helps kids flourish in their faith into young adulthood, even in the face of cultural adversity. Now, as we close this chapter, let's take a look at five ways children's ministry can become less like Disney and more like Mister Rogers.

1. Remember relational presence transcends production value.

The COVID-19 pandemic showed us that what your kids need more than something to take their minds off their pain is for you to show up and be with them in it—to tell them that you will protect them. It is so easy as parents to allow our kids to self-medicate through screens, and as kids' ministry leaders to allow the supplement of media to become a substitute for presence. But as Fred said, "Much of television is degrading. What parents give their children, though, will always be more important than what television gives them."[10]

Disney's focus is always on production value and stage presence. Fred knew that being with your kids, looking them in the eye, and calling them by name means more than a thousand YouTube videos. Production value matters in the discipleship of kids when it is used to draw them into a meaningful relationship with a caring adult. Yet if production is the means and the end, it becomes counterproductive to the process of discipleship in a child's life. In that case, what you are communicating to your children is that your job is to entertain actively, and their job is to consume passively.

Eugene Peterson defines discipleship as "a long obedience in the same direction."[11] There is nothing passive about that. It is an active obedience marked by submission to God and His Word. It is a direction that is set and a destination that is secured by the saving work of God. Discipleship is a call to obey, a call to follow Jesus. Entertainment involves us passively consuming; discipleship involves us actively pursuing.

2. Show up, listen, and insist on intimacy.

Fred understood that presence, listening, and remembering you are with them and that God is with them are far more critical than anything else. The Disney model is entertainment-driven and tries to grab *your* attention rather than give you *its* attention. Disney can only help you forget. It can never make you feel loved. Fred believed that showing up in a child's life and listening to them are some of the most loving things you can do. "Listening is a very active awareness of the coming together of at least two lives. Listening, as far as I'm concerned, is certainly a prerequisite of love. One of the most essential ways of saying 'I love you' is by being a receptive listener."[12]

One of the greatest misconceptions about discipleship is that it is primarily the transfer of information. Fred knew that children can teach us a lot. So, when you show up in a child's life, don't just show up and speak. Listen to the kids you are leading. Listen to God and His Word. German theologian Dietrich Bonhoeffer agreed with Mister Rogers when he said, "So often Christians . . . think that their only service is always to have to 'offer' something when they are together with other people. They forget that listening can be a greater service than speaking."[13] Discipleship involves presence, as we have already said, but it also involves *focus*. We must listen. Only through the power of presence and the gift of listening can we build the framework by which disciples are formed.

3. Tell your kids the truth.

Fred said we should "find the simplest truthful answers."[14] Children know when they are being lied to; they know when you are not telling them the truth. As parents and leaders who are proclaiming the truth of the gospel to kids, we must never lie to our kids.

When we tell our children the truth, we build future trust. We parent in the age of Google. If you lie to your children, they will ask Google and find out. When I was growing up, my parents could tell me anything, and I had no other choice but to believe them. We live in an information age that spreads unlimited information, much of it misleading. We must tell our kids the truth—always.

The conversations you have with your children at ages three, eight, and eleven are building a bridge to their future selves that you will need to cross when your children are sixteen, eighteen, and twenty-one—after they have been hurt by a broken relationship or find themselves at a party and are afraid. Every time you tell them the truth, you place a board on the bridge of trust that will allow you access to your children in future years.

When we give our children pat answers, they will find out. When we lie to them, we train them not to trust us and we redirect them to other sources to find the truth.

When you tell your children the truth, you reinforce what is true and they learn over time that "I can trust you." In a world of fake news and fact-checking everything, there is nothing more valuable than trust.

4. Don't forget you were a kid once.

One of our biggest challenges in teaching kids the Bible and discipling them is that we have forgotten what it is like to be a child. One of the keys to Fred's success was his simplicity and childlikeness. This came from his ability to understand and empathize with the joys and fears children face. He gained this ability through listening to kids and being present with them in a very intentional way. When asked how he learned how to do this, he responded:

> When I first started working with children at a family and child-care center, as time went on, I spent hours and hours observing and listening, and little by little, something wonderful began

to happen: I remembered how it felt to be a child myself. I remembered the bewilderments, the sadnesses, the joys, the lonely times, the angers. Having remembered these things, I found that I could make myself more available to the children I was with. I could take the time to listen to these children's needs before deciding what their needs were.[15]

When you remember what it is like to be a child, you are able to give them a faith to grow into rather than a faith to grow out of.

When you remember what it is like to be a child, you are more equipped to proclaim the gospel to your kids. You won't be inclined to simplify the gospel to the point that it's so sanitized it's powerless to incite wonder and captivate their mind and heart. But you will be free to teach all of the Bible to children—to contextualize it for them, rather than sanitize it. You are able to give them a faith to grow into rather than a faith to grow out of.

5. Keep in mind, most of all, that Jesus was a kid once.

Because the Gospels start with a thirty-year-old man, it is very easy to forget that God was a child once. Jesus was a baby who grew. But He didn't only grow physically; He grew in favor with God and with man (Luke 2:52). What a powerful and profound statement that is. To think Jesus, fully God and fully man, grew. It's important to remember this because it changes how we see every child around us.

When we think of Jesus, we think of Him as the miracle worker who walked on water, not the boy who cried when He scraped His knee. This understanding frames how we treat kids and what we expect from them. If we want our kids to grow up and be like Jesus, we have to remind ourselves that Jesus was a kid once.

Walt Disney helped kids escape reality. Fred Rogers stepped into their reality and brought hope. Walt distracted an entire generation. Fred discipled a whole generation. This generation of kids needs to be discipled in the way of Jesus like no other generation before them. My hope for us as leaders is that we have a shift in passion—a shift away from only trying to get people into our buildings toward focusing on who our people are becoming. I pray we see our need to make disciples of all nations, our need to preach and baptize, and our need to remember we don't do this alone. We can't do this alone. Jesus promised we would never be alone when He said, "Behold, I am with you always, to the end of the age" (Matt. 28:20). What a promise, what a Savior.

In the next two chapters, we are going to follow Jesus' example as we discuss the *old* and *new* maps of children's ministry. And each "map" will have three primary "cities." These cities will represent the dominant forces of influence within children's ministry. But before we do that, my coauthors and I want to create explicit clarity around what we are saying and, therefore, what we are not saying.

Acknowledgment of the major cities on the old map of children's ministry does not mean each of us (especially those of us who serve in the local church) contributed to the building of these cities, nor does it mean all attributes of these cities are incorrect. We are simply acknowledging three things:

1. These cities are the dominant forces of influence within children's ministry.

2. We have more knowledge and insight now than we did when these cities were built.

3. We need to ask ourselves if these cities should remain the same influential forces in the future that they were in the past.

As church leaders and Christ-following parents, we are critical thinkers. Church history is filled with brave thinkers who dared to ask the hard questions. Today's children need you to ask hard questions, reflect, and evaluate as we move into an increasingly post-Christian future. By going through an evaluative process, we can gain insight and then lift our eyes and dream of a preferred future—one that will shape a generation whose inner resilience is so compelling that future communities will be drawn to their Christlike beauty.

QUESTIONS FOR REFLECTION

1. In what ways can elements of fantasy, while grounded in reality, be incorporated into children's ministry to captivate their imagination without compromising the truth of the gospel? How might the balance between creating engaging, entertaining environments and imparting essential truths be struck in a way that aligns more with Fred Rogers' approach?

2. How has the cultural shift toward constant innovation and distraction affected your personal life and relationships, especially in the context of child discipleship? How can you ensure that technology and media supplement relational presence rather than serving as a substitute for it?

3. In what ways have technological advancements contributed to both positive and negative aspects of your interactions with children, and how might these influences align with or deviate from Fred Rogers' philosophy?

4. Reflect on Eugene Peterson's definition of discipleship as "a long obedience in the same direction." How can the active,

ongoing nature of discipleship be emphasized over a passive consumption mentality, especially in a culture that values entertainment?

Gaining Perspective

- What is the rate of success you, your pastor, and the parents whose children you minister to would be happy with as it relates to faith that lasts well into adulthood?

- In what ways do you/your team try to achieve those metrics? These could include programs, practices, trainings, etc.

- Have they been successful? How do you know?

• • •

CHAPTER THREE

The Old Map of Children's Ministry

—◆—

MATT: Have you ever heard of the leadership term "a burning platform"? Perhaps you've heard someone say in a meeting, "We are standing on a burning platform." Or, "We don't want to find ourselves trapped on a burning platform." But where does this term come from?

On July 6, 1988, a massive fire claimed the lives of 167 men working on the Piper Alpha oil rig in the North Sea. To this day, it's the largest number of deaths in an offshore accident. "The explosion was the result of an avoidable lack of attention—the failure to check simple systems that had been working just fine for the decade leading up to the fire. And it was intense—the blaze shot nearly 300 feet into the air, and it could be seen from about 62 miles away."[1]

This fiery term—*burning platform*—refers to the story of a worker living on the Piper Alpha who awoke one morning to a loud explosion and an all-consuming conflagration. The man stumbled to the platform's edge, where he confronted a terrifying ninety-eight-foot drop to freezing waters.

> The man on the burning platform decided to jump. The situation "was unexpected. . . ." In ordinary circumstances, the man would never consider plunging into icy waters. But these were not ordinary times—his platform was on fire. The man survived the fall and the waters. After he was rescued, he noted that a "burning platform" caused a radical change in his behaviour.[2]

That's quite jarring. It reminds me of a podcast where I (Matt) was being interviewed by Carey Nieuwhof and David Kinnaman surrounding the results of a Barna Group study we had commissioned titled *Children's Ministry in a New Reality*. During the discussion of the old map, David Kinnaman said something equally as jarring: "We know what we are doing right now isn't really working, and it's not just not working sort of, it's not working at all."[3]

Wow, David didn't mince his words. And he also wasn't finished. While talking about the fact that only 10 percent of eighteen-to-twenty-nine-year-olds are "resilient disciples" (essentially the output of the old map), David continued, "What we are doing isn't really working unless we are really happy with only 10 percent resilient discipleship output. So, even if some of the things that we try don't end up working much better, at least we are trying something different."[4]

I encourage you to go and check out the rest of the interview, but let me summarize David's concluding thought during this portion of our journey: Church leaders and concerned parents must actively evaluate what we are doing in our children's and student ministries. We need to evaluate the underlying assumptions of our local children's ministry and ask hard questions like, Is our ministry producing the outcomes we hope for? And if not, why not? What could we do differently?

When David says, "It's not just not working sort of, it's not working at all," he's describing a burning platform. But do we see it as such? Do we view the church's output of only 10 percent resilient disciples among eighteen-to-twenty-nine-year-olds as a reality we must accept? Or, do we view it as an opportunity to ask, What could we learn from these "resilient disciples" to see that 10 percent become a growing 20 percent, 30 percent, or even higher?

Ministry to young people is not producing the intended results because we're using an old map based on decades-old assumptions. As we walk through the old map of children's ministry, with its three major cities, Sam, Mike, and I would like to convey the three-part thesis of this chapter:

1. It's not a matter of *will* the church move to the new map (which is actually an ancient map), but *when*.

2. We need to thoughtfully begin charting the new map.

3. If we don't move toward the new map, we'll eventually discover the old map of children's ministry is a burning platform—and be forced to take a leap.

The Old Map of Children's Ministry

I'm by no means a cartographer. Probably like you, I know just enough to be dangerous. We know maps have a title, scale, legend, and compass. They have latitude and longitude lines, roads, major landmarks, indicators of landscape and topography, and . . . cities. And we know not all cities are created equal.

Take New York City, for example. You could say NYC is the city that influences other cities. What would Trenton, Newark, Long Island, New Haven, Hartford, and Atlantic City be without New York City? For that matter, how different would Los Angeles, Chicago, Boston,

Paris, or even Katmandu be if New York City had never existed? NYC is such a global force of influence that it has both a direct and indirect worldwide impact. It's the city that influences other cities. It's a dominant force of influence on a global scale that is undeniable.

In much the same way, City #1 on the old map of children's ministry is not only a dominant city that influences other cities, it's actually not just one city—it's a twin city. Much like Minneapolis and St. Paul or Dallas and Fort Worth are considered twin cities—two singular entities that are different from one another but function hand in hand—so are the twin cities of Church Growth and Entertainment.

City #1: The Twin Cities of Church Growth and Entertainment

The First of the Twin Cities: Church Growth

If the church growth movement were a wave, you could say the wave has crested and is now in a crashing phase. There's been quite a bit written on the church growth movement over the past fifty years. As that wave has crested and started to crash in the past ten to fifteen years, much of what has been written more recently has been more evaluative in posture. Was the church growth movement helpful? What were the strong points? What were the unanticipated consequences? And where does the church go next?

To begin answering those questions, let's put the church growth movement in context with other movements.[5] For the sake of simplification, church growth (also known as attractionalism) is one of a handful of common ways of facilitating local church implementation in the US, the others being movements like the teaching model, missional model, house church, and formational model (or discipleship). Numerous books have been written on each of these models, and there can be varying levels of Venn diagram-like overlap among them. However, the dominant model in the West by far has been church growth.

Here's a basic definition for the church growth model that our team came up with:

The church growth model is the stewardship of knowledge and wisdom to grow the church through attractionalism marked by emphasis on evangelism, missions, practical ministries, and numerical growth.

In the spirit of candor, when I consider that definition, it sounds pretty common sense to me. I mean, who doesn't want to carefully steward the knowledge and wisdom we've been given? Who doesn't want to *grow* their church? After all, Jesus said, "Go and make disciples" —meaning, "Reach and form more people in *My* image." And reaching people for Christ and meeting practical needs are really good things. So what's the problem?

Anyone who's been in church leadership for more than a couple of years knows there are two words in that definition that are the *driving force* within the church growth model, and they are the last two words: *numerical growth.*

Numerical growth is the driving force behind the attractional model to the point that it's become the *chief* metric that's influencing, forming, and shaping the behaviors of local church leaders, especially kids' pastors.

One time after I gave a keynote at THINQ Culture Summit on making the shift from children's ministry to child discipleship, I was greeted in the lobby by the kids' pastor of a well-known megachurch.[6] (You'd recognize the name of this church.) This leader was enthusiastically complimentary of the presentation I gave of the latest research we commissioned by Barna Group. As he shared with me his passion for these very same ideas as a dad and as a kids' pastor, I could also sense what was coming: *the lament*. And sure enough, he said, "I'm facing a big problem at the leadership level. Our executive pastor has given me the goal of moving our children's ministry attendance from 13 percent to 30 percent of the overall church body attendance." He continued, "Instead of asking the question, 'How can our church form lasting faith in children?' I'm in a position where the chief question I'm forced to answer is, 'How can we make kids' ministry more exciting to increase our weekly attendance?'"

If you are a church leader or on staff at a church, stories like this likely don't surprise you because the church growth model is such a dominant force of influence. It's sort of all most of us have ever known. On the other hand, if you are a parent who likely doesn't have full visibility into the inner workings of a local church, you may find this a bit shocking.

Although it is true the aspiration of the church growth model is to actually disciple more people, it can be a bit like chasing after a mist. Such an inordinate amount of energy is spent on getting more people to attend the primary, weekly church offerings that far fewer resources actually get applied toward deepening the discipleship (formation) of church attendees.[7]

On the upside, when you get more people to a local church on a Sunday morning, that's more people hearing the gospel, listening to biblical teaching, gaining spiritual insight and wisdom, and having the opportunity to learn, worship, and grow. On the downside, there's ample data indicating that showing up at a church service alone is not forming lasting faith.[8] The assumptions that most churches operate under relating to the church growth (attractionalism) model are faulty, and we've invested significantly in this approach at the risk of underinvesting in others. Simply stated, churches who place their dominant investment into numerical growth will not be truly healthy churches.

Just as cities often have a founder, the church growth model did too, and most sources credit Donald McGavran as the founder of the church growth movement. So what's McGavran's story, and how did he become so influential on the church today?

To boil a biography down to a paragraph, McGavran did his graduate work at Yale and later earned his PhD from Columbia University. He spent time on the mission field in India and various parts of Africa. Upon returning from the field, he spent years researching how mission works grow and expand at Northwest Christian College (now Bushnell University) in Eugene, Oregon, and at Fuller Theological Seminary. It was at these institutions that he was able to shape the thinking of more than a generation of not only missionaries in his program, but also another professor and colleague, Peter Wagner. Wagner began taking McGavran's ideas and principles and applying them to the US church context. It's out of this body of work that the church in America began placing increased energy into areas like evangelism, pragmatic methods, the removal of barriers, and focusing on receptive target audiences. This overall effort had a profound impact on US pastors from the 1970s to 1990s, notably leaders like Robert Schuller, Elmer Towns, Bill Hybels, Chuck Smith, John Maxwell, Rick Warren, Leith Anderson, and many others.

But the church growth movement isn't just something that impacted only well-known megachurch pastors like in this list above; it is impacting nearly all of us. Regardless of whether your place of worship is a small country church that brings in a gospel quartet to boost attendance for an annual revival . . . or a megachurch in the suburbs of a major city that brings in a Christian celebrity for an

We need more than numerical growth; we need formation that leads to lasting faith.

"Inspiring Stories Weekend" . . . most churches in the West have not escaped some aspect of the dominant influence of the church growth movement. There are certainly a lot of positives we can take away from the movement as well. However, if we equate "numerical growth" to "discipleship that forms lasting faith," we are making a leap too far. We need more than numerical growth; we need formation that leads to lasting faith.

Let me punctuate with this: Nothing has shaped children's ministry in the US more than the church growth (attractional) model, because this model has created the dominant context in which most US churches operate. This might explain the nagging feeling you and I experience quite often of, "How do I make this more fun?" or "What can we do to get more kids and families to show up?" or "How can we top last year's event?" Where do the assumptions behind those questions even come from? You guessed it. The dominant city on the old map of children's ministry: Church Growth and Entertainment.

As we move to the second twin city, Entertainment, what does it have to do with children's ministry? And, more specifically, what's the strategic linkage that formed Church Growth and Entertainment into the dominant twin cities on the old map of children's ministry? Let's travel over to it and find out.

The Second of the Twin Cities: Entertainment

As children's ministry emerged throughout the 1980s and 1990s and became a robust cottage industry by the early 2000s, we actually doubled down on fun. More than fun, *entertainment*.

Now, don't get me wrong; children are, by nature, fun. Like me, you may have had the privilege of traveling the world and observing children in a variety of contexts. Wherever I travel, I see kids—even kids with little to no resources—always finding ways to have fun. It's the delightful nature of working with children.

Think about it: What's the number one question parents ask when they pick up their child from children's ministry? Is it, "What did you learn about Jesus today?" No. It's, "Hey buddy! Did you have fun?!" It's not necessarily a bad question, but it's enlightening that it's the dominant question by far. Why is that?

In a research project we conducted in 2014, we evaluated:

A) the level of importance of different areas of children's ministry, and

B) the performance within each area.

This type of research methodology allows you to do what's called a *gap analysis*. Meaning, if we say "area X" of children's ministry rates 5.0 in terms of importance (the highest level of importance), yet we actually score ourselves within that same area at 3.5, then the "gap" between how important we say "area X" is and how well we are performing is -1.5.

In our 2014 study, there was only one area where we, as a children's ministry community, outperformed the level of stated importance. Any guesses on what it was? Fun!

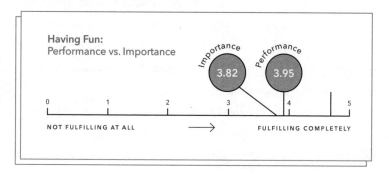

Having Fun:
Performance vs. Importance

Importance 3.82 Performance 3.95

0   1   2   3   4   5

NOT FULFILLING AT ALL   ⟶   FULFILLING COMPLETELY

"Having fun" is the only category where children's ministry leaders outperformed our rating of importance. As a community, we rated "having fun" as a 3.82 in terms of importance, but acknowledged we were actually performing at a 3.95.[9] As a children's ministry community, we not only say children's ministry should be fun—we live up to it!

After the height of COVID-19 had crested and children's ministry conferences were beginning to gather again, I found myself walking around the exhibit booth area of one such conference. I decided to play a little game and keep track of how many of the booths would fall into the category of "entertainment." This conference had roughly one hundred booths, and as I kept a running tally, two out of every three were tagged as entertainment. To be honest, 65 percent is about what I would have guessed, as this is pretty consistent with our experience.

So, how does this play out on the streets? In Peoria? In West Des Moines, Greenville, Springfield, or Decatur? Qualitatively, as I travel and meet with children's ministry leaders (and I have for more than eighteen years), this is a reality we often grieve as a community. We believe we've invested far too much into entertaining children (especially in today's culture where kids are over-entertained), and we fear that it's not yielding long-term discipleship impact in today's world.

In *Resilient: Child Discipleship and the Fearless Future of the Church*, my coauthor Valerie Bell said, "I fear we may realize too late that we gave them things that didn't really matter, things that didn't travel into their adult lives as anything more than spiritual entertainment and moralistic stories, things lacking real spiritual power and proactive purpose."[10] I think Valerie captured the lament of children's ministry leaders all too well.

So what happened here? On the back side of the church growth wave—a wave that has already crested and is crashing—we are pensive, realizing that we strategically linked entertainment as a means to stimulate church growth. In other words, if we want to grow our churches, we need a thriving children's ministry that attracts more families. (It doesn't take a rocket scientist to figure that out.) And we doubled down on entertainment to maximize the fun with kids to grow our churches. Thus the powerful twin cities were forged. This dominant force crafted a culture that has become so normative that we operate in such a way that we're not even sure how we got here. It's "just how it is." When you do children's ministry, this is the way you do it.

However, now we're not so sure this is the best way. We find ourselves, like Valerie, wondering if we've given kids lesser things that simply will not travel with them into their adult lives. We got out of bed one morning only to realize we'd awakened in a post-Christian culture that's forming kids at a rate that's outpacing our kids' ministry, or kidmin. And we're asking ourselves if City #1—the twin cities of Church Growth and Entertainment—should remain the same influential force in the future that it's been in the past.

Which leads us to the second city on the old map of children's ministry: Relevance.

City #2: Relevance

Normally, when our family travels in the car, we stream music or listen to podcasts. Yet, for some reason, on a random Saturday this past year, we wandered over to that old-fashioned medium known as "radio." Apparently, K-LOVE now has a radio station called K-LOVE '90s. Did you know about this? For real. It's a thing. Katie wouldn't switch the station. Neither would I. Listening to a mixtape of 1990s Christian music was like being back in the youth group again (which I think is their actual slogan!). At one point, the Newsboys song "Shine" played, and we heard these lyrics that we've not thought of in over a decade—maybe two! "Shine. Make 'em wonder what you got. Make 'em wish that they were not on the outside looking bored."[11]

As we were singing along (yeah, sorry), we were like, Wha?! Did we really sing that?! Yes, in the '90s we did. In the spirit of a Christian-culture postmortem, what we were saying here is essentially, "Hey you *non*-youth-group kid! You, over there bored out of your ever-loving mind and having zero fun. Look at us and the way we shine. Don't you wish you were as cool as us? Come join the fun!"

Now, to be fair, by the 1990s, this mindset of "cool Christianity" was spreading quickly. Not just the church growth model, but the missional model too. Christians wanted to be relevant. The economy had gained its footing, more people were attaining wealth, Christian music was becoming cool (*Jesus Freak*, am I right?[12]), everyone was going on mission trips, Christian T-shirts were everywhere . . . it just felt like Christians could *finally* attain coolness. There was this sense that we had the resources and the wherewithal to make Christianity relevant enough. We could make Jesus and the church so cool our friends would come to know Jesus and our churches would grow.

This pursuit of relevance wasn't only limited to the youth group or the main adult service; it was in children's ministry too. By the time 2010 rolled around, one of the big themes among children's ministry bloggers and workshop facilitators was How to Make Your Children's Ministry Spaces More Like Disney.[13] As we have touched on already, the overarching thinking was if we would model children's ministry after the way Disney did spaces, environments, storytelling, entertainment, child engagement, and more, we could be more relevant in the minds and hearts of kids and families and ultimately lead them to encounter and grow in Jesus. This narrative is still the dominant force to be reckoned with in children's ministry today, which is why it's the second city on the old map.[14]

Brett McCracken, author of *Hipster Christianity: When Church and Cool Collide*, was reflecting over a decade after his book was published and said, "That 'cool Christianity' is, if not an oxymoron, at least an exercise in futility. A relevance-focused Christianity sows the seeds of its own obsolescence. Rather than rescuing or reviving Christianity, hipster faith shrinks it to the level of consumer commodity, as fickle and fleeting as the latest runway fashion."[15] McCracken is saying that "cool" Christianity is exhausting and unsustainable. And perhaps nowhere in the church is this more apparent than in the children's wing. We chase after the facility remodel, the newest entertaining video curriculum, the latest kids' worship music, improved media equipment, updated graphics or murals for the walls, a younger kids' pastor, new volunteer team T-shirts with an updated design, and the list keeps going. Before COVID we already knew it was exhausting. Post-COVID we now know Brett is right; it's both exhausting *and* unsustainable.

In his book *Disappearing Church: From Cultural Relevance to Gospel Resilience*, Pastor Mark Sayers makes the point that in our pursuit of "relevance," the church becomes changed by the very culture we are trying to reach.[16] If we are not careful, the major drivers of our methodology can become edutainment-focused, consumeristic, materialistic, and over-preoccupied with relevance. So, instead of leveraging the thinking of Disney as a tool or resource to become more effective at engaging children for the gospel, we simply end up *becoming* Disney. We're scratching our heads, wondering, *Is this even working? Are we placing far too much effort into trying to be relevant?*

John 6 includes the famous passage in the Gospels where Jesus feeds the five thousand. In verse 56, we read Jesus saying these words that can sound so obtuse to the human ear: "Whoever eats my flesh and drinks my blood remains in me, and I in them" (NIV). I think we've all had that thought of, *Jesus, perhaps You should have run that statement by the marketing department before You let loose.* But if we read this passage intently and with a keen spiritual eye, it's abundantly clear there's a missed message taking place. Earlier in this text, Jesus was using free bread to paint a picture of His identity (the bread of life). Jesus was messaging: "Consume Me. I am the bread that comes from heaven, which needs no source. Just as this bread fills your stomachs to sustain your life, I am the source of life itself." But instead, the people of Capernaum ate the object lesson and missed the Messiah. After Jesus said that hard saying, He went on to ask the twelve disciples in John 6:67 (NIV): "You do not want to leave too, do you?" To this, Peter responded, "Lord, to whom shall we go? You have the words of eternal life. We have come to believe and know that You are the Holy One of God" (vv. 68–69 NIV).

Are we placing far too much effort into trying to be relevant?

As I contemplate the complex challenges of children's and youth ministry today, I think of this passage frequently. Jesus was beyond smart. He knew that the "free bread" message would sell. He also knew that the "eat my flesh" message could clear the room. Jesus understood the appropriate importance of true relevance: in this case, filling hungry stomachs with free bread. He also knew that His core message (I am the bread for your soul, consume Me) would be missed by many, which is why He was willing to say the hard thing.

A few years ago, the kids' pastor of a well-known, nationally recognized church was giving me and a ministry partner a tour of their children's ministry wing. As we walked along on the tour, the kids' pastor informed us about how they were inspired by Disney; they even hired Disney artists to produce the art that was on the walls. Honestly, it was so spectacular I had to remind myself I was not at a theme park or an interactive children's museum. On the way to the car, I remarked in sarcasm to my ministry colleague, "That children's ministry space is so over-the-top amazing that if I were a kid at that church I'm not so sure I'd even understand my need for Jesus."

In our pursuit of relevance, trying to make kids' ministry over-the-top cool, we fear the children in our ministries may be filling their spiritual bellies with temporal, lesser delights and missing the Bread of Life. We need to ask ourselves, like the people of Capernaum, Are the kids in our ministry consuming the object lesson, but missing the Messiah? If so, what is the object lesson they are consuming, and how is it forming them?

It appears that our love for relevance has not developed spiritual resilience.[17]

As we've journeyed the old map of children's ministry thus far, we've discussed how the twin cities of Church Growth and Entertainment form the most dominant city on the map, followed by the second city of Relevance. Now we are going to explore the third and final city: Bible Lite Strategy.

City #3: Bible Lite Strategy

As a young man I learned the phrase, "It may be accurate, but it's incomplete." This quote speaks to the idea of nuance (or subtle variances). When someone says, "Yeah, that's true, but you are leaving out an important detail," that would be an example of this idea. Nuance and subtle variances make a world of difference.

Have you seen this classic T-shirt?

Let's eat Grandma.
Let's eat, Grandma.
Commas save lives.

It's true! Nuance does save lives. Not just on a quippy T-shirt but in various facets of real life: signaling in traffic, giving skydiving instructions, determining medicine dosage, and remembering which kid has the peanut allergy. Subtle variances make a difference. And nowhere do we need to be more keenly aware of this than in the way we communicate the Bible to children. Let's unpack this together.

So, what exactly is the Bible Lite Strategy?

The Bible Lite Strategy emphasizes values, morals, or good character from the Bible in a way that's unrooted from the gospel. It isn't always inaccurate, but it is incomplete.

Good character is not the goal of a Christian; it's the by-product of a life surrendered and cultivated in Jesus Christ.

Let me give an example of how this plays out on a Sunday morning in Topeka. You are leading your large group lesson. A killer video of "Nehemiah building the wall" plays. The kids are into it. You teach the lesson with the help of your drama team, reenacting key parts. And as you are bringing it home, you say to the kids something along these lines: "Nehemiah was all about teamwork! This week, we are going to focus on teamwork. Nehemiah wanted to build a wall, but he couldn't do it without his friends. When we all work together, we can do anything. If you learn how to work together as a team you accomplish all that God has for you to do."

As you drive home from church, you wonder about the time you worked together with your friends and failed in the end. Or about the time when people worked together to build a tower to reach God, and God saw that what they were doing could be accomplished, but it would be destructive if they did. Why, when we did work together, did things not work out?

This is the dilemma of the Bible Lite Strategy.

Going back to part of the definition above, "it isn't always inaccurate, but it's incomplete," working together is knowing that what you are called to do is in the heart of God, that His strength goes with us, and that His power is empowering us. Our teams will accomplish more by the grace of God. We can accomplish more by the power of God when we are doing the will of God like Nehemiah. Teamwork is not the focus of Nehemiah's story. A God who loves, restores, and can rebuild is the focus of that story.

When what we teach is Bible Lite, we use the Bible to help us get what we want.

When we have a high view of Scripture, however, we ask what this means to them and then how it applies to us. Teamwork is important, but it's not how Nehemiah built a wall; it was built by God's grace and Nehemiah's effort. Even when we fail, it's not a failure if we trust God. God's plans never fail, so when we work to do anything according to God's will, we can be confident that God is leading us to a place that He has already prepared for us.

Do you see it? The nuance and subtle variances in how we communicate? It's right there. And when we get this wrong, the consequences for children can be significant. Actually, the Bible Lite Strategy has become tremendously popular and appealing as a way to teach the Bible to children. It's just simply not the gospel, and it's not the way the Bible was intended to be understood and taught.

So how should we teach the Bible? Take a look at this simple analysis tool our team created to help us best understand the consequences of the Bible Lite Strategy.

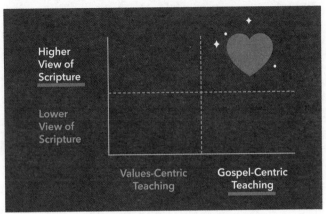

Bible Lite Strategy X and Y Axis Chart

Vertical Axis (from top to bottom): On the vertical axis you see a scale referring to how a local church views Scripture. Does your church have a high view of Scripture? Meaning, do you view the Bible as true, reliable, infallible, and God's inspired word? Or, does your church have a low view of the Bible? Meaning, you may view the Bible as a good book that's partially true, a collection of stories that may or may not be historically accurate, and filled with universal wisdom, but not completely divinely inspired or infallible.

Horizontal Axis (from left to right): On the horizontal axis you see a scale referring to how you teach or exegete the Bible. After all, there is a lot of information in the Bible; how should we parse it out in a way children can understand? On the left end of the scale is a church that teaches the Bible with emphasis on the values, virtues, character traits, or even an applicable behavior from each particular Bible story or passage. On the right end of the scale is a church that teaches the Bible as a unified, historical story of the gospel, traces the thread of the gospel from Genesis to Revelation, and teaches kids to understand Bible passages in context to Jesus, His life, and His ministry on earth and the cross.

In case the big heart in the upper right-hand corner didn't already give it away, that quadrant is where we want to encourage you to strive for as you teach the Bible to children. Not just because we say so, but because this is how the Bible itself unfolds, and as faithful Christians we can look back and see that this way of teaching the Bible is the best that two thousand years of church history has to offer: a high view of Scripture combined with gospel-centric teaching.

Sadly, when churches follow the modern fad of values-centric teaching, it erodes the biblical foundation in children and the future of the church. Let me illustrate what's happening with some practical, values-centric teaching sound bites:

- Just as Noah obeyed God, you can obey God.

- Like Abraham trusted God, you can trust God, too.

- Esther made the right choice, and you can make the right choice, too.

- As God's people cooperate together to build the tabernacle, you can cooperate with others, too.

- Like the little boy who gave his fish and loaves, you can also give to Jesus.

- . . . you get the idea.

In the values-centric teaching list above, you can see it emphasizes character formation in a way that's not only disconnected from the gospel but is also placed in front of the cross (see image below).

Gospel-centric teaching (which we will discuss further in the next chapter), however, says that because of the work of Jesus on the

Placing the Value Before the Cross Chart

cross, for those who place their faith and trust in Him, God will form them to be like Him (see image below with value after the cross). With fresh eyes, let's look at some of these value examples again, but placed *after* the cross:

- Kids, because of the work of Jesus in our lives, we can obey God . . .

- For those who trust in Jesus, He gives us the power to . . .

- Because Jesus saves us, God gives us His courage . . .

See the difference? One has limited human power. The other has the divine power of Jesus Christ because of the power of the gospel. Subtle variances in the wording. Nuance. But a world of difference.

Nuance and subtle variances make a world of difference.

An important question we should be asking is, What is the impact of the Bible Lite Strategy? In other words, what are the outcomes of this way of teaching the Bible? When we use the Bible Lite Strategy and fail to teach the Bible how it's intended, we risk leading kids to legalism and moralism on the right (conservatism), and

Placing the Value After the Cross Chart

moralistic therapeutic deism on the left (progressivism). Let's break these down.

The Conservative Outcome of the Bible Lite Strategy: Legalism and Moralism

Legalism is essentially a philosophy of living that's governed by rules or laws. It's living in such a way that the motivation for one's thoughts, attitudes, or behaviors is the keeping of a law, a rule, a value, or a moral that must not be broken. Moralism is a philosophy of living by a set of moral objectives to maintain an image of goodness or holiness, while also judging others who do not hold to the same values or morals as "lesser."

Legalism and moralism shape kids to think that the problem in life is found *outside* of oneself and is to be avoided, and the answer is found inside of oneself through a system of virtues or good morals. The gospel, however, says that the problem with humanity is found *inside* of oneself; it's our sin and rebellion, and the answer is found outside of ourselves in the person of Jesus Christ, who can cultivate us to be more like Him through discipleship.

This is how the Bible Lite Strategy manifests itself in a conservative context, and it's failing our children and harming the future of the church. A conservative church may have a high view of Scripture, but when combined with a values-centric teaching philosophy, this strategy subconsciously teaches children to think that values, virtues, and good character are the answer. That's unsustainable and the very reason we need not only the salvation of Jesus, but the grace, power, relationship, and discipleship that comes through Him and the kingdom of heaven.

Next, let's take a look at what happens when the Bible Lite Strategy is applied in a progressive church context.

The Progressive Outcomes of the Bible Lite Strategy: Moralistic Therapeutic Deism

Moralistic Therapeutic Deism (MTD) is a term coined by researcher Christian Smith in his 2005 book, *Soul Searching*.[18] One way to think of MTD is as "the religion of the air." It's the pop-culture version of a mash-up of some Bible, a dash of moralism, and a helping of secularism—all in one! The five basic tenets of MTD are:

1. A god exists who created and ordered the world and watches over human life on earth.

2. This god wants people to be good, nice, and fair to each other, as taught in the Bible and by most world religions.

3. The central goal of life is to be happy and to feel good about oneself.

4. The god of MTD does not need to be particularly involved in one's life except when he is needed to resolve a problem.

5. Good people go to heaven when they die.

By no means are Sam, Mike, and I suggesting that Sunday school teachers in Nebraska or kids' pastors in Georgia are intentionally teaching MTD in the local church. What we are suggesting once again goes back to the power of nuance—the subtle yet important differences—and how we (Christ's advocates to children) must carefully articulate how we teach the Bible in our culture of mass confusion.

Mark Sayers, an Australian pastor and author of brilliant books like *Reappearing Church* and *A Non-Anxious Presence*, helps us understand the need for clarity as he describes the dominant culture that today's children are growing up in: "Post Christian Culture is an attempt to advance the goals of Christianity without Christ. [It's] the kingdom without the King."[19]

The Bible Lite Strategy perpetuates this "kingdom without the King" idea when we unintentionally teach this generation the very same virtues the post-Christian culture is pursuing, such as justice, kindness, love, mercy, freedom, and peace, and fail to make a clear and direct connection to their source, King Jesus.

Another way of putting this is what Quaker theologian Elton Trueblood calls a "cut-flower civilization."[20] The values and virtues we teach children, like the flowers on a bouquet, look beautiful, but once cut off from their root system (King Jesus, the gospel) have a limited life span before they wither. Therefore, when we use a values-centric approach with children and teach a virtue like "goodness," yet don't articulate it clearly in relationship to its source, we are unintentionally fueling the dominant cultural narrative within Moralistic Therapeutic Deism of "God wants us to be good," and children are missing the gospel. Bible Lite perpetuates "the kingdom without the King" and fuels a "cut-flower civilization" because it simply lacks a clear articulation of the source of virtue, values, morals, and character.

Sayers and Trueblood understand that when we pursue the

outcome (the value, virtue, or moral) without a clear and direct line to the source that can cultivate the outcome (King Jesus) inside of us, we've gone the direction of a progressive and unsustainable faith. To a child or a student, popular phrases such as "love is love" or "live your truth" or "follow your heart" sound similar to messages like: "As David loved Jonathan, you can love your friends too . . ." Suddenly, the dominant cultural narrative of do-good-be-nice MTD is all wrapped up in one big messy ball of yarn alongside the values, virtues, and character being taught at church. It's the kingdom without the King . . . and a flower cut off from its source.

It's not that it's all incorrect, but it's incomplete. And in its incompleteness it's powerless. The Bible Lite Strategy in a progressive context is shaping our children to become Moralistic Therapeutic Deists. John Mark Comer said, "Progressive Christianity is a stopover on the way to post-Christianity."[21] Nuance matters. And subtle variances will save more lives.

Forging a Path Toward the New Map

Let's go back to leading Christian researcher David Kinnaman and what he shared earlier in this chapter. David and his company, Barna Group, have amassed a tremendous amount of data and insight on the trajectory of the American church. Because of this, I find his perspective worth pondering. Consider the connection point between these three related items David has shared with the church:

- First, "We know what we are doing right now isn't really working, and it's not just not working sort of, it's not working at all."

- Combine that with, "The church is woefully unprepared for Gen Z."

- And last, he shares that the church in the US is currently forming resilient disciples at a rate of only 10 percent.

Sam, Mike, and I go back to the thesis of this chapter: It's not a matter of *will* we move to the new map, but *when*. We need to thoughtfully begin moving toward the new map. If we don't, we will eventually discover the old map of children's ministry is a burning platform—and be forced to take a leap.

The next chapter is about our thoughtful journey forward into the new map. It's a map that is not primarily motivated by numerical growth, but rather by forming lasting faith. Let's journey into the new map together.

QUESTIONS FOR REFLECTION

1. Are there areas where the old map of children's ministry has influenced your church or the way you think about ministry? Describe them.

2. To what degree does the push for "numerical growth" influence the culture, operation, and weekly tasks of your church staff, volunteers, and leadership team?

3. No one wants to be "irrelevant" or "not cool" in the eyes of young people. Yet, what proof or evidence do we have that our pursuit of these methods actually forms the faith of young people? Is there something else that we should place more emphasis on?

4. How would you plot your children's ministry on the X, Y Axis Chart in this chapter? Does it tend to place the virtue before or after the cross (in terms of how you teach the Bible)?

CHAPTER FOUR

Gaining Perspective

- What is the attitude of the culture/context you serve in as it relates to the Christian faith?

- Do you sense that the prevailing attitude has changed recently, and if so, what would you point to as a means to express that and how has it impacted your ministry?

- If you could start over in your role at the church, what would you do differently?

- In a few words, write down the specific thing or things that best reflect present and future success.

• • •

Charting the New Map

—◇—

Spoiler alert. The new map is an ancient map.

MATT: As Bob Webber once said, "The road to the future runs through the past."[1] And as people of the ancient way, we know this to be true. Hindsight, after all, is a gift to the wise, as we look backward to inform how we move forward.

A couple of years ago, I was volunteering in our sons' youth group. As students were breaking the huddle, my sons were headed off to that post-youth-group cultural norm known as Taco Bell. Clearly, they didn't want their old man around. So, as I hopped in the truck, I was feeling a little Elton John (just one of those days, I guess). Cueing up the *Greatest Hits* album, I pressed play, put the truck in drive, and took off. About three songs in, "Rocket Man" came on. You likely know this song, as it's been part of the soundtrack of our multigenerational lives in recent decades. Perhaps you've heard it while shopping in a store, belted it out dozens of times on a road trip, or like me, you may just be an Elton fan.

Nevertheless, it's remarkable how something you've heard, something you've sung dozens or maybe even hundreds of times, can suddenly *gift* a spiritual epiphany right into your lap. At one minute and fifty-one seconds into "Rocket Man," Elton John sings, "Mars ain't the kind of place to raise your kids."[2]

I heard that and thought, *What did he just say?* I backed it up and listened again. Repeat. Ohh. That's brilliant. This one line! This line of music that I've heard and sung over and over throughout my lifetime has suddenly given me new insight. Elton John nailed it! Raising kids today feels a lot like we are raising our kids on Mars compared to just a couple of decades ago. But he wasn't finished. In the next three lines, the lyrics go on to describe loneliness and isolation, neglect and abandonment, and how we are in over our heads with technology that we do not fully understand.[3] It's quite fascinating and even prophetic how this song that was likely written in the shadow of NASA landing on the moon and was published in 1972 could so accurately describe a post-2020 world. The road to the future most certainly does run through the past.

There's a lot that you and I would likely not see eye to eye on with Elton John, but when it comes to this, he and Bernie Taupin (his friend and lyrics writer) were right. Mars is not the kind of place to raise our kids. It's unsustainable. Yet it's exactly where we find ourselves today.

In this chapter we are going to press onward to the new map of child discipleship. As we do, we will first take a brief look at how the recent past has shaped the broader cultural landscape shifts taking place now—and how these shifts are shaping our children in alarming ways. Maps use keys, specific vernacular, and icons that serve as language to help sojourners understand how to navigate in the real world. This next brief section will give us that same clear, common language around the broader landscape shifts so we can navigate the new map with maximum cultural understanding.

Language Gives Perspective on New Terrain

As mentioned in chapter 1, the value that a map brings to its user is an accurate representation of the real terrain to help you navigate correctly and arrive at your intended destination. What good does it do you to use an outdated map that doesn't account for a new suburb that has emerged, earthquakes that changed traffic patterns, or old bridges that have been moved?

In the church in the US, we sometimes "operate" as if we are still navigating the old terrain of the past decades, but in reality, the cultural landscape has shifted (and in some cases, these shifts have created a significant change). I emphasize *operate* because most of us *know* cognitively that the cultural landscape has shifted, but we can still operate functionally off the old maps in our daily work patterns. And there's a difference between *knowing* some particular insight and allowing that insight to actually transform our perspective.

A starting point in forging the new map is an accurate understanding of the actual, real landscape of today's world, as well as additional intelligence on where the world is headed in the years ahead. In his 2018 book *Christians in the Age of Outrage*, Dr. Ed Stetzer gives us a mapping of a major demographic shift that has occurred in our cultural landscape in the US over the past seventy-five years or so.[4] The chart below not only helps us see where we've been in recent decades but also where the cultural demographics of the US are headed in the decades to come.

In this chart, the three vertical columns represent the past, present, and future. In the far-left column (the past), from top to bottom, we see four general demographics of people:

- Non-Christians—which includes those from other religious groups as well as all secular or non-believing people,

- Cultural Christians—those who claim to be "Christian" by cultural or familial affiliation,

- Congregational Christians—those who are members of a church, but who may only attend infrequently, and

- Convictional Christians—Bible-believing, united in the Apostles' Creed, life centered around Jesus Christ, engaged in a local church, etc.

The primary point Stetzer is helping us see here is that there has been a major demographic shift in terms of cultural dominance. In the past, the dominant culture in the US was what's called a quasi-majority Christian culture. Just a few decades ago, there was a mainstream respect for Judeo-Christian thinking and values. Even if there wasn't "agreement," there was at least a tolerance, if not a respect, for Christianity. The church held a place of prominence in the community, and the Bible was a well-respected book. Jesus was generally viewed as a positive historical figure, and Billy Graham was the ideal human being. There was a common understanding of the meaning of "marriage." You could simply say that Christianity held a seat at the mainstream cultural table.

But today? Not so much. A shift has already taken place, and the dominant cultural inertia is headed toward increased secularism.

As a result, today we are experiencing a cultural divide between convictional Christians (those who are defined by the Scriptures, orthodoxy, etc.) and those who may call themselves Christian (such as cultural and congregational Christians) but who more closely identify with a secularist or post-Christian worldview. If we were to use our mapping analogy to try to explain this phenomenon, we might say we've allowed the foundational concepts of the map—distance, scale, terrain, even true north—to be redefined in culture. You can imagine the difficulty that it would create to try to navigate the same region off completely different maps with wildly differing reference points; yet with people claiming to be "Christians" on both sides of the increasingly widening cultural divide, this is the disorienting reality our children are experiencing. The true north of biblical orthodoxy and two thousand years of church history have been replaced, by many, with the humanistic views and values of secularism. All the while the children we serve are trying to make sense of reality amid this linguistic and cultural chaos.

We see real value in this chart by Stetzer because it helps us gain perspective on two key insights as we chart our new map to disciple the future of the church.

Insight One: Secularism is here, and it's likely here to stay. The dominant culture of today and the near future is a secular culture. No matter how much we shelter our children, the broader, mainstream culture they live within is secular or post-Christian in its thinking. If we are fish, this is now the water in which we swim.

Insight Two: Therefore, our job as church leaders and parents is to prepare them to thrive in their faith in these new cultural realities. Our focus as their pastors, leaders, shepherds, and mentors must shift to a child discipleship process that is robust enough to form lasting, resilient faith in our new realities.

To reiterate, if we were using a forty-year-old map that did not take into account the shifts in the geological terrain, or the man-made changes in roadways, or the explosive growth in population, our perspective would be completely off. We'd be kidding ourselves in terms of arriving at our destination.

In much the same way, the map we are using to disciple our children must correspond to the *real* landscape of today, not a nostalgic, no-longer-existent cultural landscape from our past memories. Proper perception is necessary to take prescriptive action and set accurate direction; it's true for driving and it's also true for discipleship.

The old map of children's ministry simply does not take into account these seismic shifts in our cultural landscape. If the church in the US continues to view children's ministry primarily through the "attractional" lens with emphasis on entertainment and cool, Disney-like relevance, combined with the inadequacy of the Bible Lite Strategy, we will discover too late the incongruence of the old map as we arrive at an unintended destination. But we don't have to wait until a burning platform forces us to take a leap. We can thoughtfully and intentionally journey forward based on a new map that corresponds to our realities that

> The motivation at the center of the new map is love—love for Jesus and love for others.

will lead children into a thriving, Christlike future.

I suspect that as you navigate this chapter, you too will discover that what is propelling us forward—away from the old map toward the new map—is not only the logical analysis of chapter 3, but the love and hope that characterizes every aspect of the new map. The motivation at the center of the new map is love—love for Jesus and love for others. It's brimming with hope. And it's the pathway forward to forming faith.

The New Map of Children's Ministry

Following the same rhythms established in chapter 3, the new map of children's ministry is simply using "maps" as a metaphor from which we can learn and imagine together. This new map's story will also have three primary cities, just as the old map does. The first city on the new map, much like New York City, is also the dominant city that influences the others.

I enjoy visiting world-class cities. In my line of work, I've had the privilege of traveling to several cities we might view as dominant global powerhouses. There are the usual US suspects like New York, Chicago, Los Angeles, Dallas, Houston, Miami, Seattle, or my personal fave . . . Nashville. But I've also visited other dominant cities like Seoul, London, Tokyo, Kathmandu, Nairobi, Montreal, Prague, Bergen, Vancouver, Abidjan, and Munich.

Each one of these cities is a powerful force within their region of the world (and in many cases, far beyond). These cities are not aimless entities devoid of will. Rather, they are cultural manufacturers designed to shape their inhabitants in their likeness and to export their cultural product to their spheres of influence. Chicago, for example, is a city of order, systems, hard work, deep-dish pizza, education, and even groupthink. Nashville, on the other hand, is a city of relational networks, entrepreneurialism, collaboration, individual-ism, and my least favorite aspect, mass chaos on the interstate. Bergen, Norway, is a city of no noise pollution, no billboards, inner peace, and outdoor exploration. And Los Angeles is about entertainment.

Every dominant city is also asking a question. Chicago, a city of systems and neighborhoods, is asking, Where do you fit? Kathmandu, balancing the tension of Buddhism and Hinduism in the shadow of the Himalayas, is asking you to be one with the mountain. And in the last chapter we discussed how the twin cities of Church Growth and Entertainment are asking, How can we numerically grow our church?

Then, on the new map, there's the twin cities of Faithfulness and Lasting Faith. This new emerging city is asking what I believe to be the most strategic two-part question on the planet, and it's this: What is it the church community does that forms lasting faith in children? And how can we do it faithfully?

Notice the distinct difference between the *motivation* of the dominant city on the new map compared to the dominant city on the old map.

Motivation of the *Old* Map Dominant City: *numerical growth, size, quantity*

Motivation of the *New* Map Dominant City: *forming faith, depth, quality*

City #1 on the new map of children's ministry, the twin cities of Faithfulness and Lasting Faith, is a dominant force. But it's not a city that's trying to use its cultural power simply to attract more people, sell more coffee, or get you to buy a movie ticket. It's seeking to answer the question, How do we form kids with lasting faith in Jesus Christ? And how can we do this faithfully for generations to come?

At the heart of this city is the greatest invitation of love, and there is nothing that could bring us more hope as church leaders and parents.

City #1: The Twin Cities of Faithfulness and Lasting Faith

The First of the Twin Cities: Faithfulness

Faithfulness is the means by which lasting faith in Jesus is formed. The starting point in discipling the next generation is by simply participating with God as an apprentice to Jesus Christ. As we pilgrimage onward toward God, we invite the young people in our lives along on this same pilgrimage to Him. This is faithfulness. And it's the first of our twin cities.

Going back to our origin story, as in *the* origin story of all humanity, we find Adam and Eve deciding between trusting God and trusting themselves. They opted for the latter. And we humans are still struggling with this today. We opt for rebellion, disobedience, abdication, pleasure, omission, and even distraction . . . almost anything but faithfulness. But as God's loving grace wears His children down over time, we often come back to Him as humbled prodigals and see that His solution—His way—is the best and most life-giving way to experience the pilgrimage of life. His way is faithfulness.

Remember the song from childhood, "Trust and obey, for there's no other way, to be happy in Jesus, than to trust and obey"? What is this? It's faithfulness. Jesus says,

> "Enter through the narrow gate. For wide is the gate and broad
> is the road that leads to destruction, and many enter through it.
> But small is the gate and narrow the road that leads to life, and
> only a few find it." Matthew 7:13–14 (NIV)

My friend and pastor Jim Nicodem says, "If God is the source of Adam's life (and of ours), what would be the natural consequence of unplugging from God by rejecting His commands? Death. Isn't that what happens when you're vacuuming your house and the plug pulls out? The vacuum dies, right? Well, people who unplug from God—the source of life—die."[5] Faithfulness is the daily pursuit of plugging into Jesus Christ and His kingdom. Faithfulness is the ancient path. The narrow way. The light and life. You and I, we tend to rebel, we sin, we struggle, we give in to temptation, and we also have our victories—all while faithfulness teaches us to walk in repentance and humility in the grace of the gospel of Jesus Christ.

Perhaps no one has described this journey better than Eugene Peterson in his book *A Long Obedience in the Same Direction* (Sam referenced this book in chapter 2). Peterson writes, "We are people who spend our lives apprenticed to our master, Jesus Christ. We are in a growing-learning relationship, always . . . we are people who spend our lives going someplace, going to God, and whose path for getting there is the way, Jesus Christ."[6] This "long obedience in the same direction" that Peterson is describing here is faithfulness. It's the way.

As we journey forward on this long obedience, when we look around we notice that we are not alone. There are children all around us—at home, at church, at school, and in our community. They are watching us closely, and picking up what we are doing.

Katie and I decided early on in our marriage that, when appropriate, we wanted our sons to have a front row seat to experience the lows of life alongside us. At times, this meant that we had a disagreement with them in the room. At other times, this meant that we were navigating a challenge with a friend, family member, or coworker, and we did not shield them from the details. Both Katie and I have been to therapy to heal and overcome past challenges and traumatic experiences, and we have intentionally invited the boys into these healing types of conversations with thoughtful nuance. Furthermore, when we wronged the boys in any way, we've tried to model humility, repentance, forgiveness, and responsibility. Although careful nuance must be applied in each of these examples, we decided to parent in this way for one reason: faithfulness. We wanted Warren and Hudson to grow up in a home where faith was not an annex to our lives. It was the way.

Faithfulness is one of those attributes of the Christian faith that's central. And it's often caught . . . not taught.

Children need to be able to see, hear, and experience the essence of faithfulness so they actually know what it is. Faithfulness isn't only something on the pages of Scripture; it's the hand next to a child in the car on the ride to school. When a mom allows her daughter to be beside her in the pain of a mundane Monday in the car line at school as mom is battling out some struggle with God, this mom isn't "telling" her about Proverbs 3:5–6, she's living it! She's tangibly experiencing faithfulness in a way where her daughter can not only see this is the way—she can catch it.

Kids catch this not only from their parents but also from pastors, kids' pastors, teachers, volunteers, coaches, and mentors.

But what are they catching? What does it look like?

In his book *The Ruthless Elimination of Hurry*, John Mark Comer describes living out faithfulness as an apprentice to Jesus this way:

1. Be with Jesus.
2. Become like Jesus.
3. Do what Jesus did.[7]

This is what we want every parent to long to embody for their children. To be with, become like, and do what Jesus did. This is how we walk out our discipleship. This is faithfulness.

Want to form the faith of the next generation? Faithfulness is the way. As pastors, ministry leaders, and spiritual shepherds, we not only train and equip our volunteers and parents to live out faithfulness with kids; it's who *we* are as spiritual leaders ourselves. Who wants to see another pastor fall in the news headlines? No one. What can prevent this? A life cultivated in faithfulness to Jesus Christ. This is our first responsibility in forming the faith of the next generation—to be faithful ourselves, and to model this faithfulness for parents and children through the grace of Christ. This is the first of the twin cities of Faithfulness and Lasting Faith.

Now we're ready to move on to the second of the twin cities on the new map of children's ministry: Lasting Faith.

But First, a Brief Note to Parents of Prodigals

In any given setting I'm in, I'm regularly reminded of the number of spiritual prodigals represented. Parents and grandparents, you may have done many things correctly. Or, you may lament mistakes and regrets. The pain is real. I'm reminded of what Davis, Graham, and Burge said in their book *The Great Dechurching*,

> Having this heavenly city and this compassionate Savior and his Spirit as our Great Comforter, we have no need to trivialize what is lost when people leave the church (especially when they are leaving in droves). We don't have to pretend they weren't true friends or that it didn't hurt or that we were perfect and it was all their fault. This greater comfort allows us to acknowledge and sit with the gravity of grief that rightfully accompanies the Great Dechurching, since we have this hope as an anchor for our souls. It allows us to own our responsibility for the departing, whatever that may be, knowing that our shame and our punishment have been borne by another. Despite even our worst failings, the

church will be presented as a spotless bride when the King returns for her (Eph. 5:27). That's not because her (and our) sins weren't real; it's because they were really paid for (Isa. 1:18).[8]

Discipleship isn't a magic formula or a silver bullet. Faith formation is, however, a lifetime pursuit. It truly is a long obedience in the same direction. Like how the water of a river smoothes the rough edges of a rock over long periods of time, so is the life of a Christ follower. Jesus changes us, little by little. We place our hope and trust in Him as we humbly live out our discipleship journey. And along this journey, we petition to Him, we contend with Him, we even wrestle with Him, that He would bring the hearts of our prodigals home. The pain and grief you feel is real, and is not to be diminished. The biblical hope that we have is to trust God, live in Christian community, delight in Christ, and remain faithful.

The Second of the Twin Cities: Lasting Faith

By 2013, we, at Awana, began asking, "What is it the church community does that tends to form lasting faith in kids?" To this day, this is still the central question of our global ministry. This is our passion, our core competency, and our area of expanding expertise.

When we first started down this path, what we were actually trying to understand was this: If you were to take away all of the surface-level methodologies and tactics—all of the entertaining elements of children's ministry like funny videos, adorable puppets, Disney-like environments, goofy skits, exhilarating games, creative Bible teaching, colorful graphics, boys-against-girls competitions, engaging songs, etc.—what are the objective factors behind those methodologies that we can prove correlate with forming lasting faith?

We do a lot of things in children's ministry, but for many of these tactics, we can't truly prove that they are causal or even correlative in child faith formation. So, after we set those types of items aside, what are the known factors that are causal or correlative to forming lasting faith? This is what we wanted to understand. Because if we can understand this and share this insight with the church, we can help churches globally become fruitful stewards at forming the faith of the next generation.

So, in our pursuit of answering this question, here's what we've been up to the last decade:

- Careful observation of how Jesus made disciples in the Gospels

- Nine Child Discipleship research projects (quantitative and qualitative), including one with the Barna Group titled *Children's Ministry in a New Reality*

- An additional three robust "Impact Studies" by *Excellence in Giving* on the effectiveness of our child discipleship ministry in the US and in parts of Africa and Southeast Asia

- Gathered research from LifeWay, Barna Group, Fuller Youth Institute, Christian Smith, and others

- Vast study on the broad discipline of discipleship

- Qualitative reports, emails, and newsletters from our missionaries all over the world

- And seventy-four years of dynamic ministry learnings

In our passionate pursuit, we centralized all of this research, followed the insights, and distilled them down to the primary factors that are most known to form lasting faith in children. We discovered that there were three. We call these primary factors that shape faith in kids *Belong*, *Believe*, and *Become*, aka the 3B model. It looks like this:

Child discipleship is designed to *form lasting faith*
by helping kids *belong* to God and His kingdom,
believe in Jesus Christ as Lord and Savior,
and *become* like Jesus and walk in His ways
through the power of the Holy Spirit.[9]

Here is how these factors are defined individually:

- **Belong:** highly relational ministry led by loving, caring adults

- **Believe:** deeply scriptural ministry rooted in the gospel and the truth of God's Word in order that kids may know, love, and serve Jesus Christ

- **Become:** truly experiential ministry designed to help kids navigate a changing culture, experience God's presence, and walk in the ways of Jesus[10]

In the clearest language possible, what we see here is that *Belong* is about making sure children have consistent relational engagement with loving, caring adult disciple makers. *Believe* is placing children in environments that are rich with consistent Scripture engagement. And *Become* is helping children to experience the practices of the Christian faith as they navigate the world around them. What is this? This *is* the process of forming faith. This is child discipleship. These are unmovable objectives by which you can build a holistic strategy to influence child faith formation. These objectives exist to inform and shape our methodologies, our programs, ministries, and various activities.

For a brief moment, let's compare "child discipleship" (as defined above) to what we traditionally call "children's ministry" and "family ministry."

In the US we tend to think of "children's ministry" as something that takes place at church on a Sunday morning, or perhaps one evening a week. Not that we necessarily think of the impact as being limited to that time and space, but in terms of the methodologies, those activities do take place at a particular time (e.g., Sunday morning) and at a place (e.g., the children's ministry wing). Churches in the US invest heavily in cool and inspiring spaces, engaging dramas, funny videos, elaborate puppets, creative Bible teaching, awesome graphics, fun games, inspiring worship songs, volunteer T-shirts, and easy-to-use media and curricula. Many of these are valid methodologies that are mostly connected to a time and place that make up our shared understanding of children's ministry, and how the activities of children's ministry operate. I should also state that none of the above are inherently wrong—kids should absolutely find joy in church—but these means often receive an outsized measure of our attention and resources.

Then there's "family ministry." Family ministry is the pursuit to train, equip, and resource parents to reach and disciple their own children at home and as they go about life throughout the week.[11] The hope and aim behind family ministry is that parents will engage with their own children in discipleship activities like conversation, prayer, Bible reading, family worship time, discussions about culture and everyday life, faith conversations, memorizing the Bible together, as well as modeling for their children humility, repentance, and other Christlike attributes.

The big insight here is that child discipleship provides a super-structure by which church leaders can build and align a children's ministry and/or a family ministry.

Child Discipleship

Children's Ministry   Family Ministry

The 3B child discipleship approach isn't just about church (children's ministry). It isn't just about home (family ministry). Child discipleship is about viewing child faith formation as a holistic effort—one in which loving, caring adults (volunteers and parents) are trained and equipped to engage children in ways that are most known to form lasting faith in children.

In other words, children's ministry is designed around what takes place at church. Family ministry is designed around what is supposed to take place at home. Child discipleship is designed around the child's holistic and realistic life experience. Therefore, child discipleship informs how we build our children's ministry and our family ministry. *Belong, Believe, Become* creates a thoughtful approach to child faith formation. It's not a program or a set of methodologies, but rather unmovable objectives for how we approach holistic child faith formation. When the church and the family both understand this remarkable insight, they can work together on a new map, which is really an ancient map, to influence the lasting faith of children.

Some additional nuance we need to notice as church leaders is that this isn't about just any *one* factor. It's about when all *three* factors take place simultaneously. When a child experiences the combination of belonging, believing, and becoming, he or she has the best opportunity to begin and build a personal relationship with Jesus Christ as a child or youth disciple.

Perhaps no other youth faith formation expert has expressed these factors more clearly than well-known researcher Christian Smith, who wrote, "No single factor can produce high levels of emerging adult religiousness. Instead, multiple combinations of factors working to-gether are necessary to more likely than not produce that outcome . . . every most-likely path to highly religious emerging adulthood must include combinations of *distinctly different kinds* of causal factors, al-most always including groupings of relational, personal-subjective, and devotional-practice factors." Smith then defined the necessary variables of those factors as "strong, personal **relationships** with adults who bond teenagers to faith communities (either parents or supportive non-parents), strong expressions of subjective teen per-sonal faith commitment and **experience** (high importance of faith, few doubts, many religious experiences), and . . . high frequencies of religious practice: (prayer and **Scripture reading**.)"[12]

Smith's research here is almost identical to ours. Again, it's not any one factor, it's when the multiple factors of relationships (*Belong*), Scripture engagement (*Believe*), and experiences (*Become*) create a dy-namic combination of multiple factors working together. This is the focused, intentional pathway to form lasting faith in young people.

When I talk to the average kids' ministry director, they know this. We *all* know—whether intuitively, subconsciously, or intentionally—that relationships, Bible engagement, and experiences (or practices) work together to form the faith of children and youth. I don't think our problem is a knowledge gap. Rather, it's an operational hard-wiring problem. A tactical or methodological problem. The week-to-week binding realities that "Sunday comes every week" and "I gotta keep the children's ministry machine crankin.'"

Truth be told, as I've already given a nod to, our functional weekly reality looks a lot like this:

VBS/SUNDAY SCHOOL/YOUTH GROUP/LARGE GROUP/SMALL GROUP/COMMUNITY GROUPS MIDWEEK/STAFF MANAGEMENT/VOLUNTEER MANAGEMENT/VOLUNTEER RECRUITMENT STAFF AND VOLUNTEER TRAINING/KEY CHURCH RELATIONSHIPS/BUDGETING AND PLANNING BUSINESS MEETINGS/AND THE SEEMINGLY ENDLESS NUMBER OF SPECIAL EVENTS

Don't Burn It All Down

In children's ministry we feel stuck as we are trying to spin more plates than we can reasonably expect to keep spinning. Inevitably, a plate will come crashing to the floor, as this pace is impossible. That shattered plate may be a failed event, not enough capacity to make something successful, lack of attendance, fewer volunteers for a particular program, losing connection to your kids or your spouse, or you're at the doctor's office because your body is taking the toll and it's telling you to slow down. All of these are symptoms that the old map is failing us. Like clues, they are telling us that something is amiss.

Perhaps, for some, the temptation is to scrap it all. To tear everything down and take a match to it. Wisdom, however, tells us that a "burn it all down" strategy is foolish and irresponsible. That's not our path forward. To be honest, there are many good methodologies on this list above.

Yet, lasting faith does not start at the "methodological" level; it begins at the "objective" level. Relationships, Bible engagement, and experiences are unmovable strategic objectives that can be applied to numerous tactics, methodologies, programs, and ministries.

93

In the meantime, don't burn it all down. But begin to chase after the vision of what we know tends to form lasting faith. And as you travel down this path, remember: faithfulness is the way.

You don't have to go it alone either. Do this with your team through dialogue, collaboration, planning, and prayer for a preferred future—one that's built around the primary factors most known to form lasting faith. Real craftsmanship takes time and a guiding coalition of your core leaders in collaboration. Don't shortcut the process. Instead, build a sustainable ministry that is centered on what's most known to form lasting faith in kids—*Belong, Believe, Become.*

> As you travel down this path, remember: faithfulness is the way.

Many churches continue to chase after numerical growth, yet hardly a week goes by where we don't hear about another church leader who has fallen in this effort. It seems as if our pursuit for "bigger" is leaving us hollow on the inside. I'm trying to think of a time when Jesus was wringing His hands because He wanted a larger group. Rather than going after numerical growth, may we be faithful as we turn our chief efforts to what's most known to form lasting faith in kids.

Faithfulness and Lasting Faith—that's the dominant twin city of children's ministry on the new map. As those who shape the faith of children, this is our highest objective. It's what we build our local church ministries around—to form the lasting faith of children. This is the driving motivation behind City #1.

Now let's take a look at City #2: Community.

City #2: Community

A while back I read an article in The Gospel Coalition by Pastor Brian Bowman, who leads and shepherds Valley Life Church in Phoenix, Arizona. The article, titled "I was Discipled by . . . the

Church," contains some powerful insight for those who aspire to shape the future.

Brian's article reads as a chronological overview of his childhood, skimming from his third grade Sunday school teacher, to a friend's dad who mentored him when he was in eighth grade, to a conference he attended in ninth grade, and on into his young adult years. Today, Pastor Brian has concluded that he was discipled by "the church." What does he mean by this? He means there were multiple loving, caring adults who discipled him during his childhood and teen years. It wasn't a single moment. It wasn't a particular mentor. It was the collective impact of several relationships within the community of the church that discipled him and shaped his faith.

What's contained in Pastor Brian's article is what research shows to be the most *catalytic* factor in forming childhood faith: community.

As a researcher in child faith formation, I think Pastor Brian is a genius. He understands that relationships are the catalyst. This is exactly what came through in our research with Barna Group, which says, "Today, two in five churched parents of 5-to-14-year-olds (39 percent) indicate their child has a meaningful relationship with an adult at their church."[13]

**Two in Five Children in Children's Ministry Have a
Meaningful Relationship with an Adult**

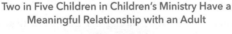

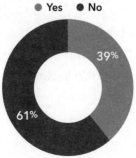

n=1,021 U.S. churched adults with a child ages 5-14 at home, June 11-July 6, 2021

So this is a good news/bad news story. The good news is that 39 percent of the children in our local church ministries have at least one loving, caring adult at church whom they feel connected with relationally. The bad news is that 61 percent do not. Clearly, the church has room for improvement.

The real insight, however, is in the cross-tabulation as we drill further down into the data. As you look at the following two charts, notice the difference between the kids who have a meaningful adult relationship at church and those who do not.

The story here is this: *it's not even close.*

Kids who have access to "at least" one meaningful relationship with a loving, caring adult are far more likely than their peers to actively engage in their own faith formation.

This whole idea of the positive impact that just one adult can have on the life of a child (let alone an entire engaging church community!) is not unique to the Christian community. In a study on *resiliency* in children, the Harvard Center for the Developing Child concluded, "No matter the source of hardship, the single most common factor for children who end up doing well is having the support of at least one stable and committed relationship with a parent, caregiver, or other adult."[14]

I can still remember the day my father walked out on our family. I was sitting on the floor facing my bedroom door, which was wide open. My father was screaming and yelling up and down the hallway carrying out cardboard boxes as well as clothes on hangers draped over his arms. Back and forth he'd go up and down that hallway. My older brother did all that he could to distract me by sticking the Disney Golden Books in front of my face. But no amount of distraction could cover up the carnage of that day. In my little world, this was like a bomb going off, and even though I now live hundreds of miles away, I'm still picking up all those little pieces.

Parents of 5–14-year-olds:
Thinking about how your children interact with church and children's ministry, how much would you agree or disagree with the following?

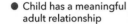

% strongly agree

● Child has a meaningful
  adult relationship

● Child does not have a
  meaningful adult relationship

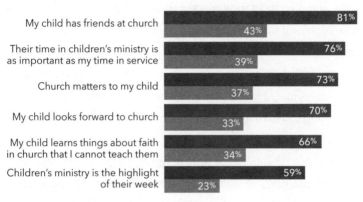

My child has friends at church — 81% / 43%

Their time in children's ministry is as important as my time in service — 76% / 39%

Church matters to my child — 73% / 37%

My child looks forward to church — 70% / 33%

My child learns things about faith in church that I cannot teach them — 66% / 34%

Children's ministry is the highlight of their week — 59% / 23%

n=1,021 U.S. churched adults with a child ages 5-14 at home, June 11-July 6, 2021

Parents of 5-14-year-olds:
Thinking about your child and their experience at church, how true are the following about them?

"My child..."
% say "completely true"

● Child has a meaningful
  adult relationship

● Child does not have a
  meaningful adult relationship

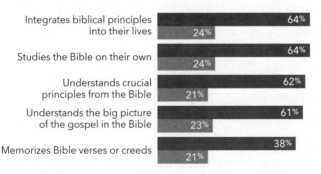

Integrates biblical principles into their lives — 64% / 24%

Studies the Bible on their own — 64% / 24%

Understands crucial principles from the Bible — 62% / 21%

Understands the big picture of the gospel in the Bible — 61% / 23%

Memorizes Bible verses or creeds — 38% / 21%

n=1,201 U.S. churched adults with a child ages 5-14 at home, June 11-July 6, 2021

In the days that followed, my mother found her way to a local church. I can still see the children's ministry wing in my mind's eye as if I'm still in the room. Off to my left there's a bank of windows and it's pink outside. This tells me it was likely a Sunday or Wednesday evening. There are only four people in the room. There's a child to my right, and directly in front of me a man and his wife. The kind, gentle man is playing songs like "Jesus Loves Me" on a guitar. Quite humble and simple. Yet, this is where, for me, it happened. Jesus met me that day and called me to Him as a little boy. All I can remember is that this Jesus sounded far better than my father and I wanted Him. As the Holy Spirit called to me, I trusted Christ as my Savior on that day and began to take my first steps of faith.

The years that followed were marked by engaging Sunday school teachers, moments of children's ministry flannelgraph lessons, baseball tournaments, struggles at school, church softball games, after-church potlucks, youth group Bible lessons, ongoing verbal and emotional abuse from my father, Wednesday night prayer meetings, spiritual gifts assessments, church choir productions, dating, high school football, church camp, and adventurous family vacations with my mom and my stepdad.

Like Pastor Brian's experience, the people of the church were like a thread that wove through the long, slow journey from childhood into my upper teen years. There was Kevin the children's church leader and Larry the deacon and Mike the youth pastor and Kimbol the pastor and Nancy the note-writing encourager, just to name a few.

Like Pastor Brian, the people of the church discipled me.

There was no master plan. Just a relationally rich environment where Jesus was at the center of it all.

A 2022 study by the Springtide Research Institute introduced what's called The Belongingness Process. This is the process of helping a child or a young person move "from *noticed* to *named* to *known*." Just this week one of my children's ministry friends shared a story in which he asked some kids, "If you could have anything, what would you want?" and one child privately shared with him that he just wants his family to notice him.[15]

What's interesting about this devastating story is that the child didn't even say he wanted his family to "know" him, he simply wanted them to "notice" him . . . the first step in the process.

If we are not careful and intentional about moving from the old map to the new map of children's ministry, we may keep bringing an abundance of entertainment and a cool-vibe relevance to a generation of children who have been oversaturated in entertaining media and simply need someone to notice them. To know their name and to understand their world—someone who makes them feel *known*.

As a church leader, a pastor, or an influencer in your church community, you are in a position to shape a local church culture that is highly relational, where kids are noticed, named, and known. Today's kids need this! In a culture of mass confusion, more and more children and teens are turning to TikTok, Instagram, YouTube, or Reddit to get answers to their questions. Instead, they need relational translators and advocates walking beside them to help them understand how to love and follow Jesus in the midst of a warped and crooked generation.

This is the future of children's ministry: a church that's primarily motivated by faithfulness and forming lasting faith in children. And the most catalytic way to form lasting faith is to cultivate a local church community where volunteers, parents, pastors, and congregants engage kids through a highly relational church culture.[16] Although many kids grow up in homes where Mom and Dad participate in discipling them, most simply do not. We want these kids to be able to say, "I was discipled by . . . the church."

No other entity in your geographic area is poised for *community* quite like your church is. The church is built for this unique moment. Now is our time to shine.

Next, the third and final city on the new map: Gospel and Scripture Engagement.

City #3: Gospel and Scripture Engagement

We are at a moment in church history where the church is sensing the need to shift from *attractional* to *formational* ministry.

The new map—an ancient map—is designed to help us make this shift. Its true north is found in the gospel, and its scale, distances, and distinct elements are informed by orthodoxy, church history, and the power of the Holy Spirit. It's a map to help us navigate both where the world is today and where the world is headed. It's a map motivated by faithfulness and the primary investments that are most known to form lasting faith in Jesus. One of the major contributions to forming lasting faith is what we just covered in the second city, *community*. The other major contribution is the *Gospel and Scripture Engagement*, the third city on the new map. Let's take a look.

In today's world, a child has to process information in a confusing context. Let's compare these phrases directly below:

At church a child may hear . . .	Outside of church a child may hear . . .
"Love your neighbor."	"Self-love is the greatest love."
"God's Word is the source of truth"	"Live your truth."
"Your identity is in Christ."	"You be you."
"Love the sinner, hate the sin."	"To not approve of me is to hate me."
"Do not kill."	"My body, my choice."
"Be kind to others."	"Your opinion of me is hateful."

What's happening here is two forces at play: Cultural Formation on the right, and Gospel Formation on the left. Tragically, children today spend most of their time in a world of cultural formation where these counterfeit narratives are the dominant story. Essentially the names we give these prevalent narratives are naturalism, secularism, post-Christian culture, hedonism, hyper-individualism, digital capitalism, and even in some cases, cultural Christianity.

If a child is spending most of his or her daily life saturated with these counterfeit narratives, how does this impact the way they interpret the world around them?

For example, what do love, kindness, truth, and identity even mean to this generation? Cultural formation is such a powerful force that it is distorting the very meaning of these important words and ideas. The result? Confusion. Chaos. Instability. Anxiety. Isolation. We find it difficult to even have a common language, not only with children and youth, but with other adults in our world today.

So, what do we do about this? What should children's ministry leaders do differently to maximize our effectiveness and fruitfulness in our new world? This brings us squarely to the first part of the third city, the gospel.

Today's kids need to hear the gospel, and they need to hear it with clarity and consistency. Not simply the salvation message, which is the climax of the gospel. They need the complete message of the good news of the gospel because most of today's children are unaware of the biblical narrative of creation, fall, redemption, and restoration.

Why is this so important?

When I was growing up in the 1970s to the 1990s in a highly Christianized farming community in Middle America, it was assumed that there was a creator. We knew we were sinners and were aware of a God who could save us, but quite frankly many people just lived in rebellion of these truths. When we sinned, we knew we were sinning, and we tried to hide it. This historical dominant cultural narrative was at a minimum theistic, and in many cases biblical in nature. Although the experience in places like San Francisco, Boston, LA, and New York may not have been quite the same as flyover country, the fingerprints of the impact of Christianity were a part of the cultural narrative of recent decades in the US.

Those fingerprints have faded with time.

Some have debated whether today's American children are growing up in a post-Christian culture, or possibly in a pre-Christian culture characterized by increasing biblical illiteracy with each emerging generation. I'll save this debate for the scholars. Either way, the vacuum today's kids are experiencing is most certainly devoid of awareness of the fullness of the gospel, which is:

Creation: God is the one true God and He has always existed. God is the Creator of all things, including you and me. He is good, He loves us, and we are made in His image.

Fall: Adam and Eve sinned and disobeyed God. Sin broke the world, and people were separated from God. People could not fix their sin problem on their own.

Redemption: God sent His Son, Jesus, to die on the cross, to take the punishment for our sins, and to rise from the dead to conquer death. When we trust in Jesus as our Savior, our relationship with God is made right again through His grace, and He gives us new life.

Restoration: When we walk with Jesus through the power of the Holy Spirit and by feasting on God's Word, He renews us. One day, Jesus will return to renew all things.

In his book *A Creative Minority*, Jon Tyson writes, "The gospel should surpass any competing story, but many Christians are only living out part of the Good News, which gives rise to paralyzing doubts." He continues, "Yet many Christians have been taught only half the story—that we were born sinners and our focus should be on getting ourselves and others to heaven. To bypass the notion that we were made in God's image or His desire for restoration of the world is to miss crucial parts of His loving story for us."[17] Especially in pre- and post-Christian cultures, kids need the full context—especially in light of all of the competing narratives. To not give them the full narrative is to undermine the message of the Holy Bible.

By giving children the full context of the gospel narrative—with clarity and on a consistent basis—we are helping them in three primary ways.

1. The gospel gives children reality.

Kids need to know what's real. Secularism is desperately failing our kids because it's counterfeit. The gospel will not fail them because it's reality. What's real is that humans were created. Adam and Eve trusted themselves rather than God and brought sin into the world through their rebellion. We all face this same curse today. Only Jesus can save us from our sins, and He can slowly restore us through discipleship to Him—and one day He will restore all things and people to perfection.

This is what's real. And kids need to hear this true biblical narrative. Over. And over. And over. Why? Because it's reality.

2. The gospel points children to salvation from sin and death.

Kids need to know that Jesus is the answer to their sin and death problem. The secular world contradicts itself by sometimes saying, "Sin? What sin?!" At other times it weighs young people down with ever-changing cancel-culture legalism that's impossible to live up to. The gospel helps children to understand where sin comes from, what it is, who can save them, and what to do about it. The gospel of Jesus Christ is our salvation from sin and death.[18]

3. The gospel shows children how to live here on earth.

Kids need to know the road to salvation. Fact. But the gospel doesn't stop there. The gospel of the kingdom of heaven that Jesus preached helps kids know how to live . . . now. Today's kids are watching secularism implode upon itself. The attempt to renew humanity apart from God is a complete and utter failure. The gospel of the kingdom of heaven that Jesus talks about in the Bible will not fail children.

Jesus shows children how to live . . . today. His ways are true, and they are the best way to experience life on earth.[19]

So, great insight. Good information. But what do we do with this?

We make it central to all we do. Make it clear. And repeat it. The gospel narrative (creation, fall, redemption, restoration) must become central to all that we do in children's ministry. Children need to hear this true, biblical narrative with clarity and consistency. Every quarter. Every month. Every week.

We cannot repeat this beautiful, compelling, and true narrative enough—because it's what's real, it's what leads to true salvation, and it's the only way to experience true life on earth, now.

If we fail to make the gospel narrative clear to today's children, we can expect many of them to become overwhelmed by the sheer volume of the unrelenting false narratives of counterfeit cultural formation. The impact of this will further our sobering and devastating reality.

Let's go one step further.

When kids have clarity around the gospel narrative *and* consistent Scripture engagement, we are giving them the best opportunity to form lasting faith.

> When kids have clarity around the gospel narrative *and* consistent Scripture engagement, we are giving them the best opportunity to form lasting faith.

Let's think about this for a moment. Imagine two children in our children's ministry: one who grasps the gospel narrative, another who only knows the dominant cultural narratives. How will these children each hear, understand, and interpret the following teachings in our local church children's ministry?

The story of Noah

The story of Moses

Bible lesson on the virtue of kindness

The story of Daniel

Bible lesson on the virtue of honesty

David and Goliath

Bible lesson on the virtue of love

The story of Esther

The Parable of the Prodigal Son

Bible lesson on the virtue of courage

The story of Stephen or Paul or Peter, etc.

The child who grasps the fullness of the gospel narrative—creation, fall, redemption, and restoration—has biblical context. I would even say, this child has *reality* context. This child doesn't view the Bible as a collection of random stories or virtues. Rather, this child views the Bible as the source of reality. The Bible becomes deeply meaningful to them because they are able to align the individual stories and virtues to the superstructure that the gospel provides. This context allows everything to "click." Suddenly, the Bible aligns. It makes sense. It's one consistent story. The story of reality.

For the child who does not grasp the gospel narrative, as they are listening to the Bible stories, lessons, and virtues, how are they processing this information? They are hearing it in the context of their view of the world, the "counterfeit reality" as it's told to them by the world. And if their view of the world is through the lens of the dominant cultural narratives, then how will they process a lesson on the virtue of love? The virtue of kindness? The various epic stories from the Scriptures? Logically, they will hear and process these stories through their forming worldview—a worldview that's quite secular. A worldview that's counterfeit.

Our kids need virtues . . . they need Bible lessons . . . but they need to know and understand them in the context of the narrative of reality—the gospel.

Kids need Scripture-rich environments, at church and at home. This is the most fruitful way to form faith in children. But even for the kids who only get access to the Bible at church, when we give them various ways to engage and get access to the Word in the context of the fullness of the gospel, we're providing the best opportunity to ignite a resilient faith in Jesus Christ.

To be sure, the world is working overtime to feed them a counterfeit narrative. So when we give children the real narrative of the gospel and consistent ways to engage the Bible, we are giving them the most foundational investment known to form lasting faith.[20]

A 30,000-Foot View of the New Map

So, let's do a quick recap of all we've covered on our journey together navigating from the old map to the new map. The old map is trying to answer the question, How do we grow our ministries? In the simplest language possible—the old map is about *numerical growth*. Maybe not intentionally, but certainly in how many churches "operate." Yet here's what we now know: It's almost as if we are raising this generation of children and youth on Mars. We're no longer living in the 1980s, '90s, or even the early 2000s. We're living in a new, highly secularized world, and it's aggressively shaping children as they grow and develop.

In this new world we live in, our children are suffering from two simultaneous failures.

One, the secular vision of utopia is completely failing our children.[21]

Two, the attractional approach to local church ministry is also failing our children—the overemphasis on entertainment and cool-type relevance is simply not robust enough to form children with a resilient faith in Jesus Christ in our highly secularized context.[22]

Mars is not the ideal environment to raise children, but it's where we seem to find ourselves. We need a sustainable approach to child faith formation for today's world (and where the world is headed). So we must let go of the nostalgia of the recent decades of children's ministry and grab hold of a new map—one that's built around the formation of lasting faith. And here's what this map looks like:

Faithfulness and Lasting Faith

Community

Gospel and Scripture Engagement

This map is a healthy, new perspective.

It's ancient, rooted, yet it also takes into account the unique needs of today's children. For us as church leaders, this is our map as we lead into the future. This is our blueprint to participating in the Great Commission in our age. These are the strategic objectives that can influence the faith formation of the children and youth in our ministries in our new highly secularized, post-Christian world. As much as we long for the nostalgia of the past, that world no longer exists.

Today's children don't need the outdated methodologies motivated by numerical growth. They need a pathway that influences and forms lasting faith in Jesus Christ. They need gospel formation. They need child discipleship.

The shift from attraction to formation ministry is taking place right in front of our eyes. As church leaders and pastors, we can either lead the shift, or the shift will lead us. Those who choose to not shift to the new map will quite likely eventually find themselves standing on a burning platform—eventually being forced to take the leap.

So why wait?

QUESTIONS FOR REFLECTION

1. In your local context, how is the culture forming children today in ways that are different from when you were growing up?

2. What would you say is the aim or mission of your children's ministry? How well do you believe your mission supports the formation of lasting faith in children?

3. How important are community and relationships to children in your local context? What two or three things can you do differently to become more highly relational with children to help them know they belong to your community?

4. What cultural narratives are forming the hearts and minds of kids in your community? What can your church do differently to make the gospel story (creation, fall, redemption, restoration) abundantly clear to children?

Intermission

✦

CONGRATULATIONS! You made it to the halfway point. Thus far on our journey together we've traversed from the old map to the new map. Along the way we see a faith-formation pathway emerging that focuses on the timeless objectives of Faithfulness and Lasting Faith, Community, and Gospel and Bible Engagement. These are the unmovable objectives by which we form the faith of children—in a children's ministry, at home, and in all of life.

With this timeless map to guide us, we now head out on the second half of our journey. As we do, we look around to see who is with us on our trek, and we begin to notice parents—some who are "with us" and others . . . not so much.

For many pastors and kids' ministry directors, seeing parents engage in the discipleship of their own children is not only a deep spiritual longing, but also a deep ministry frustration. We feel like we've tried and tried to inspire them, but most parents simply do not engage. This whole endeavor of "family ministry" and equipping parents feels . . . stuck.

In many ways, you could say this topic has become our elephant in the room.

Ivan Krylov was a Russian poet who lived in the eighteenth and nineteenth centuries and penned fables. In "The Inquisitive Man," he writes about a gentleman who walked through a museum and noticed many small details but "didn't notice the elephant in the museum."[1]

In the local church, it can be easy to go through the seasons of children's and family ministry, noticing all the familiar details but failing to seek greater visibility on what parents are—or are not—doing in the process of forming the faith of their children. Our mission statements boast phrases like "partnering with parents" as we distribute resources (physical and digital) on a consistent basis in hopes that parents are taking a leadership role in engaging their kids in faith conversations, Bible readings at home, and nighttime prayers.

But are they?

In Part 2 of *Forming Faith*, we are going to dig deeper into the partnership between the church and the home. Although this is a topic that has been written about widely over the last twenty years or so, frankly we see flaws in some of our communal thinking. Assumptions that need to be challenged. And gaping holes in research that has yet to be commissioned.

Our aim in Part 2 is to put forth a strategy to partner with parents in a way that closes these gaps and fixes our shared challenges on a systemic level.

The new map of children's ministry moves beyond "attractional" ministry (numerical growth) to *formational* ministry (child discipleship) and provides us a fresh opportunity to rethink:

What does a church that forms children
as young disciples look like?

and

How can we influence and shape the home
to be a formational home?

As we proceed, Sam, Mike, and I will not only clearly define our elephant in the room, but also provide practical and thoughtful solutions with the Church Leader's Forming Faith Pathway to inspire, train, and equip parents to build a culture of discipleship in their own home—one that prizes forming faith and places Christ at the center of all things.

Let's journey into Part 2 together.

CHAPTER FIVE

Gaining Perspective

- Knowing kids will eventually age out of your ministry and therefore the time is limited, what is the most important thing for you to impart to the children? This could also be asked as, What is your goal for each child who grows up in your ministry?

- At what age does your church or ministry begin to strategically disciple children?

- Make a list of those tactics and when they begin in your church.

. . .

Our Single Most Strategic Opportunity

—✧—

MIKE: High school graduation. It is one of the few remaining rites of passage we still widely recognize in our twenty-first-century Western society. Even when other such milestones are in decline—for example, the number of sixteen-year-old drivers has dropped from around 50 percent in the 1980s to 25 percent in 2020,[1] and marriage rates are down from where they were a decade ago—high school graduation remains a significant milestone and the beginning of a new era for students as they either enter the workforce or head to college/university/trade school.

Take a moment and put yourself back there. You're dressed in a cap and gown. There are speeches about the years of childhood and high school, recalling memories, and addressing challenges. Others are speaking about the future, quoting the Dr. Seuss book *Oh, the Places You'll Go*, speaking to the promise of possibility and the exciting times that lie ahead. While some might look into the future with trepidation, most graduates look forward to the world beyond high school with wide-eyed excitement.

However, if we were to take an informal poll among pastors, youth pastors, and Christian parents in twenty-first-century America, it would be safe to assume that high school graduation is not only an occasion to celebrate but the end of an era. And for the youth pastors and parents, it can serve as the end of their student's guided faith journey—almost as if it's a perceived discipleship deadline. After all, we often hear the now all-too-familiar story of post-high school students losing their faith. Films like *God's Not Dead* only highlight the perceived threat that the faith of our young people will encounter in the world of liberal arts colleges and universities.

To be sure, the numbers we often quote are hard to ignore:

"70 percent of youth stop attending church and start leaving when they graduate from high school."[2]

"Lifeway Research found 66 percent of churchgoing teenagers drop out for at least a year between the ages of 18 and 22."[3]

"1 in 3 young adults say they go to church less than they used to pre-pandemic, a bigger portion than other groups."[4]

The threat of our children losing faith after high school looms like a great white shark in the depths of the sea when one looks out from the shore, and anyone who is raising kids, loves kids, or ministers to kids feels it. Oftentimes in the church we operate as if we are all working together to prepare young people for the discipleship deadline of age eighteen—high school graduation. It's in this season that we aim to commission students into the next phase of life to be Christ's ambassadors and advocates on their college campuses and in other pursuits. But even in the most intentional of churches, it rarely feels like we've done enough to prepare them.

The Tell-Tale Heart

In Edgar Allan Poe's short story "The Tell-Tale Heart" (which I'll do my best to recount without spoiling it for those who've not read it), the narrator is haunted by the sound of a beating heart. This sound starts quietly but grows louder and louder and more consistent. Eventually, the persistent pounding drives the narrator mad.[5]

For many who give thought to the faith of high school students, graduation day can seem like the tell-tale heart of Poe's story. The fear of our children walking away from Jesus as they walk onto the campuses of colleges and universities can seem at first far-off, but as it gets closer and closer, that fear becomes more pronounced, more regular, until it can begin to drive us mad, insane, and insecure with fear of the future and its toll on the faith of our children.

So while graduation day can be the end of an era for seniors about to head off into the world, it can also seem like the potential end of Christian faith as we think about the students leaving our church youth groups. Many churches and youth ministries pray and commission graduating seniors, entrusting them and their faith to God. It can feel seemingly powerless, like sending a ship off into stormy seas. Yet Matt, Sam, and I would contend that graduation day isn't the deadline to sow into the faith of children in our churches. The deadline for faith formation is much, much earlier than seventeen or eighteen years old.

117

The Holy Spirit Clause

It is only biblical and right to acknowledge that God is sovereign in all things, including how He draws people to faith in Jesus through the power of the Holy Spirit. While we are about to speak to faith formation and the importance of a biblical worldview in children, we do so knowing that the Spirit can and will move in ways that defy our expectations and perceived patterns. God can and does work beyond the "norms." Let us not mistake observation for objective truth, especially as it relates to how and when salvation is at stake. God is in control of all things, including the faith of children and youth, yet in His sovereignty, we still hold responsibility.

Moving Back the Deadline

Regarding how we treat those about to graduate, we should absolutely pray for and commission high school seniors. They should be set up for as much success and strengthening of their faith in Jesus Christ as we could possibly facilitate. However, we shouldn't start thinking about the potential challenges to their faith in January of their senior year. This would be like cramming for a test, which *could* result in a good grade, but seldom produces actual knowledge. While many young people do leave the church, this isn't just a youth ministry issue.

According to a study by George Barna, "What you believe by the time you are 13 is what you will die believing."[6] While perhaps a bit dramatically stated and even morbid, the truth of the matter is that the faith of that seventeen-year-old senior was largely formed by the time they were a thirteen-year-old eighth grader. High school is largely about testing limits and fortifying identity, not necessarily forming identity and establishing limits. That work begins much earlier. Some faith traditions and denominations view the middle school years as a time to confirm faith through classes and first communion. So, is middle school the time when we need to be sure that faith in Jesus Christ is ready for adulthood? Yes and no.

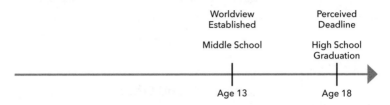

Consider the following from George Barna: "A person's moral foundations are generally in place by the time they reach age nine. While those foundations are refined and the applications of those foundations may shift to some extent as the individual ages, their fundamental perspectives on truth, integrity, meaning, justice, morality, and ethics are formed quite early in life. After their first decade, most people simply refine their views as they age without a wholesale change in those leanings."[7]

> "A person's moral foundations are generally in place by the time they reach age nine."

Words like "generally" are helpful because Barna isn't saying this is a hard-and-fast rule or an absolute. A "moral foundation" or worldview is *generally* laid before most kids hit double digits. This means those concerns about the graduating senior losing their faith as a college student when a professor or peer begins to push their theology aren't a high school ministry problem, nor an issue for middle school ministry (frankly, their jobs are hard enough). Rather, a nine-year-old's worldview foundation has already been poured, and the cement is starting to dry. Again, if we wait, even to only the middle school years, to begin the work of discipleship in the kids of our churches and families, we've waited too long.

So when should we start?

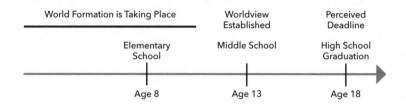

Disciple Early and Often

The faith of the graduating high schooler is the matured, Christian worldview of the middle schooler, which is built upon the foundation of the ten-year-old fourth or fifth grader, whose footings were dug in the early childhood years. When should we start? As soon as possible! Even before a child comes to saving faith in Jesus, we can begin the process of discipleship by allowing Jesus to be present in our lives, our language, our behaviors, our conduct, and our conversations.

I'm writing this chapter while sitting at the Awana office location in suburban Chicago. This morning, when I arrived and was making coffee (thanks to our COO, we have a legit coffee area), I was speaking with Miss Linda, our office coordinator and someone in whom the love of Christ radiates in her service and joy. I've known Linda for over a decade, but this morning I asked her about her salvation story. How did she come to faith?

Linda told me that when she was three years old, she was singing "Away in a Manger," and the grace and love of God through Jesus became beautiful and real to her. While her parents were nominal Baptist and Catholic, Linda would walk to her neighborhood Lutheran church, where loving, caring adults helped her know Jesus and the Scriptures more and more. Now, not quite eighty, Linda has walked with Jesus for decades, but that journey started at three years old. Some might question whether a three-year-old can make a declaration of faith in Jesus, and Linda asked this question too, but I find comfort in her words: "I don't know if I was saved at that point, but I was seen, I was called, and I became committed."

There is a reason, a divine design, why God included language of children and childhood throughout the Scriptures. From the establishing of God's people when He commanded that children needed to be engaged in the Great Shema, throughout the wisdom literature of the Psalms and Proverbs, to Jesus' blessing of children and Paul addressing his letters to the churches of the New Testament and their kids, God doesn't desire that we begin discipling kids when they're teens, but much, much earlier! Many scholars believe that the disciples were not the old men seen in the paintings of the Renaissance, but more likely they were teenagers called by and following their rabbi, Jesus of Nazareth, to become more and more like Him.

Don't Delay Discipleship

Maybe your story is similar to Linda's. Maybe you came to saving faith as a child. Statistically, many do. "The International Bible Society indicated that 83% of Christians make their first commitment to Jesus between the ages of 4 and 14, thus when they are children or early youth."[8] Friends, allow those numbers to tell the story. More than four out of five believers come to saving faith in Jesus before age fifteen!

Over the course of the research studies we've conducted regarding the importance of child discipleship, perhaps none has so clearly illustrated the need for intentional discipleship among children like the one in partnership with Barna, *Children's Ministry in a New Reality.*[9] Of the thousands surveyed, when asked, "Across the course of your life, have you been discipled at any of the following age ranges?"

churched adults (those who indicated that they were not children's ministry leaders) specifically and overwhelmingly were discipled in their childhood and teen years. According to the research: 42 percent were actively discipled from seven to twelve, 45 percent from thirteen to seventeen, with a sharp drop-off in the post-high school ages. Even though the overwhelming percentage of discipleship in churched adult lives happened from seven to seventeen, the fact that less than half of them had been discipled at all (per the data) should sound the alarm as a sobering wake-up call to the fact we need even more intentional child and youth discipleship.

Across the course of your life, have you been discipled at any of the following age ranges?

● Children's ministry leaders   ● Churched leaders

	0-6	7-12	13-17	18-21	22-25	26-35	36-45	46-55	56-65	65+	Never
Children's ministry leaders	35%	53%	67%	62%	59%	57%	43%	23%	14%	6%	3%
Churched leaders	17%	42%	45%	27%	20%	20%	17%	10%	5%	2%	13%

So let's take a moment to consider, in light of what we've covered here together, the deadline of effective child discipleship in order that mature faith may take root in the soil of the hearts of the children we serve.

- More than 80 percent of Christian children come to faith in Jesus between ages four and fourteen.
- A person's moral foundation is in place by age nine.
- The worldview of many is solidly in place by age thirteen.
- Yet, over half of all young people stop attending church once they graduate.

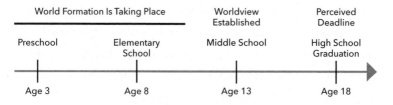

Friends, child discipleship cannot be left to chance or hoped for through hype and excitement. The deadline isn't high school graduation. Discipleship dictates worldview, so our deadline isn't even thirteen; that's far too late to begin the critical work of discipleship. Reality is defined by most people by age nine, and that script isn't written overnight. We cannot cram discipleship; faith must be formed through years and years of relationships, biblical engagement, and in the presence of loving, caring adults. It is said you cannot make old friends. Likewise, faithful followers of Jesus aren't simply made at a conversion experience; they are formed and forged, crafted and cared for, over years and years. So, church leaders, pastors, and parents, we must begin this work as soon as possible.

If those whom we disciple were a tree, like the metaphor used in Psalm 1, we would examine how the tree looks and the fruit it produces, and in doing so would make an informed judgment regarding the tree. If the fruit we're harvesting is that of young people leaving the church once they leave our ministries, I would graciously compel you to ask what that says about our churches' approach to discipleship. Fruit on the branch is seldom bad when the tree and the roots are healthy. If we want better, healthier, and stronger fruit, we need to tend to the tree and the soil. We can't treat the fruit, only the tree.

Likewise, if we want healthier and stronger disciples leaving our youth groups, we need to tend to the roots of faith formation. The three of us (Matt, Sam, and I) would implore you, ministry leader, to not wait until high school or even middle school to take seriously the work of discipleship. Child discipleship is the work of establishing roots of faith in the lives of the children of our churches. This is serious, joyful, wonderful, and important work. It's also critical and crucial because the fact is that the deadline for faith formation is real, and it's much, much earlier than we had thought.

Preaching to the Choir

If you're involved in children's ministry, this chapter may not have been all that revelatory. In fact, you may already know much of what we've written, which may have been what led you to minister to kids in whatever capacity you are. But for many in the church, this is a new and potentially sobering insight. We operate and certainly talk as though age eighteen is the deadline, but faith formation is happening much, much earlier. Our hope is that this chapter would serve as both a hopeful reminder about the important work that you already do, and a helpful resource that you can share with others. If you have influential people in your church community who could benefit from this insight, consider having them read this brief chapter.

The deadline for faith formation is real, and it's much, much earlier than we had thought.

QUESTIONS FOR REFLECTION

1. When does your ministry make a concerted and intentional effort to disciple the students in your church?

2. At what age did you come to faith in Jesus? If it was as a child, what prompted you to do so, and if you're now an adult, what factors allowed you to stay faithful past high school?

3. What are some practical ways your ministry can begin or strengthen the work of child discipleship?

Gaining Perspective

- Revisit that horizontal line you drew prior to reading chapter 1. Redraw the same line with "church" on the left and "home" on the right.

- In light of what you have read so far, replot the point indicating where on the spectrum the burden of child discipleship falls.

- Did that point change? Why or why not?

- What can you do to help the church *and the home* succeed in their discipleship efforts?

• • •

CHAPTER SIX

Getting Unstuck from Our Stalemate: Moving from Declaration to Dialogue

—◇—

MATT: Life is filled with all sorts of stalemates.

There are the big ones of the geopolitical sort. These are the kinds of stalemates that dominate the headlines, history books, and documentaries: stalemates like Alexander Hamilton and Thomas Jefferson, the numerous opposing parties of the Korean War, or Ukraine and Russia (at the time of this writing).

We also see stalemates in literature, entertainment, and sports. Stalemates like Samwise Gamgee and Gollum, Terrell Owens and the Philadelphia Eagles, the House of Montague and the House of Capulet (*Romeo and Juliet*), Wile E. Coyote and the Roadrunner, and of course that most epic office stalemate of all time, Jim and Dwight (*The Office*).

But most stalemates in life do not achieve epic status. Most are more subtle than what appears on the cover of the *New York Times*, the home page of ESPN.com, or in classical literature. Furthermore, not all stalemates occur between two "opposing" parties. The most common are like the couple sitting across from you at a dinner party who are obviously quite cold to one another. You wonder to yourself, *Did something happen in the car on the drive over, or has this been developing for some time?* Then there's the two siblings who wake up one day in their forties who begin to ask themselves, "Why are we still fighting?" When we find ourselves in a stalemate, we feel . . . stuck.

According to the *Collins Dictionary*, a "stalemate" is a situation in which neither side in an argument or contest can make progress.[1] The *Cambridge Dictionary* defines a stalemate as "a situation in which neither group involved in an argument can win or get an advantage and no action can be taken."[2] And in a rousing game of chess, a stalemate is a position counting as a draw, in which a player is not in check but cannot move except into check.

Stalemates are relational in nature. They involve two (or more) parties. And they are distinctly characterized by the nature of "being stuck" or "gridlocked."

When it comes to forming the faith of our children, God's two agents of formation, the church and the home, seem to be stuck. Gridlocked. Truth is, in most cases we're stuck in a church and home stalemate. And we've been stuck in this stalemate for quite some time. God's agents of formation are not opposed to one another, yet in many cases we can't seem to advance in our relationship and mission.

As a senior member of the children's ministry, family ministry, and child discipleship community, I was starting out in ministry in the early 2000s around the time when George Barna published *Transforming Children into Spiritual Champions*. It was in this seminal work that George popularized this sound bite that many children and family ministry leaders still use today: "Parents are the primary spiritual influence on their kids."

George Barna's exact words were, "Parents should provide the **primary** spiritual training of children. The parents may receive encouragement, training and resources through the Church, but parents are intended by God to be the **primary** provider of spiritual direction and care" (bolded emphasis mine, here and directly below).[3] His research on child discipleship was punctuated in a follow-up book published in 2007, *Revolutionary Parenting*, which also said, "Revolutionary Parents earnestly accept the role of being the **primary** and dominant spiritual mentor of their children. Most of them acknowledge the importance of being active in a healthy community of faith, but they also define that community's role as one of supplementing what the parents are doing."[4]

These were exciting times, as George Barna backed up what children's and family ministry leaders all knew (and felt!) to be true with *real* data. This work legitimized children's ministry in a way that few others had accomplished. In a way, you could say that George Barna solidly put children's and family ministry on the map, especially in the world of pastors and church leaders. His research on the discipleship of children gave children's and family ministry a seat at the church leadership table because the strategic importance of reaching and discipling humans in their most formative and receptive years could no longer be ignored.

As of the time of our writing this book, it's been twenty years since the popularization of this message that "Parents are the primary spiritual influence on their kids." It's our responsibility to pause and reflect long enough to evaluate how we're doing. For the brave and the courageous like you, we are now asking, "What sort of progress has been made in the church and home partnership over the last two decades?" Perhaps the following story from a friend of mine named Corey can shed some light on our current status.

Corey (whose name I've changed) is a kids' pastor I've known for almost twenty years. He's just a couple of years older than me, and he's been doing children's ministry for about twenty-five years. Corey has read both of George Barna's books referenced earlier, and has attended Orange Conference, D6 Conference, and Children's Pastors Conference multiple times each. He's spent the last twenty years championing Barna's message that "parents are the primary spiritual influence over their kids" in multiple churches of various sizes. He's given his life to the cause of family ministry and child discipleship, yet he recently told me, "I've spent over twenty years championing family ministry. I've told parents they are responsible to disciple their own kids until I was blue in the face. I've hosted parent events where less than 10 percent of the parents show up. This family ministry thing feels stuck. What am I missing?"

Corey is describing the stalemate. And he's wise to be asking, *What am I missing?*

Although he is a unique person, made in the image of God, this stalemate aspect of his story isn't all that unique. It's quite common, actually. We know this to be true from networking with other ministry leaders, reading books, listening to podcasts, talking with other parents, and from fresh research we will cover in this chapter.

Our latest research tells us that church leaders long to see kids grow and develop with lasting faith in Jesus Christ.[5] Our research *also* tells us that parents want to see kids formed as growing young disciples. So what gives? Why do so many churches struggle with forming a healthy, functioning partnership with parents who are engaged in discipling their kids? Why are we stuck in a church and home stalemate?

What Did George Barna Actually Say?

Let's take another look at those two prior George Barna quotes. As George's language became more influential and was packaged into the sound bite of "Parents are the primary," it became *the* mantra of children's ministry. But let's go back to the original language and the original *meaning* of the language. It's important to point out that George Barna was clear in his research and analysis not only that "Parents are the primary" but also that there are *two* agents of formation, church and home, and each has a *role* to play. According to his own words:

> **The church** is responsible for "*encouragement, training, and resources*" and must be a "*healthy community of faith*" that is "*supplementing what the parents are doing.*"

> **The home** is the place where parents provide "*spiritual training of children*" as well as "*spiritual direction and care,*" where they are the "*spiritual mentor of their children,*" and where "*parents may receive . . . training*" from the church.

It's important to point out that in the second book these were the "revolutionary parents" George Barna was researching and discussing. These were the top performers, the straight A students, the heads of the class. Reality check: these are not most parents.

So, to apply the most valuable insight and wisdom from his research in context to a broader audience—all Christian parents in a local church context—I think the following two short paragraphs of exposition provide a fair summary:

> **The role of the church** is to *train* and *equip* the congregation to disciple children and youth at home. The church does this through inspiration, encouragement, and hands-on training opportunities

for parents and caregivers to learn and gain experience so they can confidently know *how* to actively participate in the discipling of their own children.

The role of the parent is to be a disciple who engages in training and equipping provided by the church. A trained parent has the vision, confidence, knowledge, and experience to know *how* to actively participate in the discipling of their own children.

Could it be that we have swung the pendulum *so far* toward the message of "Parents are the primary"—emphasizing that "they" are responsible—yet missed the profound responsibility that we as church leaders have in *training* parents? This question has haunted Sam, Mike, and me for the last few years, and it's what led to the groundbreaking research we will cover in this chapter.[6]

In the pages ahead we will explore the analysis of *why* we are stuck in a stalemate with fresh research insights around the real sticking points. But we will not stay in the world of analysis; we are going to move beyond assessment and evaluation into what we believe are the real strategic and practical solutions that will get us unstuck from our stalemate.

Pastors and Parents Do Not Agree: Setting the Stage for the Stalemate

Imagine this scene. You're a kids' pastor, and you are at a conference on the East Coast. You are hanging out in the hotel lobby at 10 p.m. after a long day of general sessions, workshops, and far too many hours walking through the overcrowded aisles of the exhibit hall. You are one of ten church leaders sitting in a circle, and someone asks, "Who do you think is primarily responsible for discipling children . . . the church? Or parents?"

Hold that thought; let's skip to another scene.

At that very same moment, there's a group of ten married adults at a dinner party on the West Coast at 7 p.m. As they are wrapping up appetizers, sitting around an intimate dining room table, someone asks, "What do you think about our pastor's comments on spiritual parenting this past week? Do you think we as parents are responsible for discipling our kids? Or is that the job of the church?"

How do you think these two conversations would shake out?

We wanted to know the answer to these questions as well. So, in our 2022 research with Barna Group titled *Children's Ministry in a New Reality*, we asked children's ministry leaders, parents, and congregants the following question:[7]

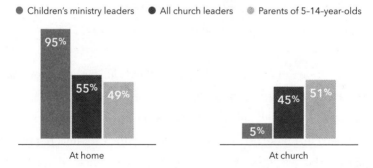

Where should the primary source of children's discipleship take place?

● Children's ministry leaders ● All church leaders ● Parents of 5-14-year-olds

95% — 55% — 49% (At home)

5% — 45% — 51% (At church)

n=600 U.S. children's ministry leaders, June 8-August 16, 2021;
n=2,051 U.S. churched adults, June 11-July 6, 2021;
n=1,021 U.S. churched adults with a child ages 5-14 at home, June 11-July 6, 2021.

According to the data, our two imaginary conversations could not look any more different.

The Declaration from Children's Ministry Leaders

The ministry leaders talking on the East Coast are likely to agree that they emphatically believe the responsibility for the domain of faith formation belongs in the home. To be explicitly clear, a response rate of 95 percent isn't just a yes . . . it's a "heck, yes!" with lots of exclamation points and emojis. There's no dialogue happening here, it's a *declaration*: Parents are responsible for discipling their own children. Period.

The Dialogue among Parents and Congregants

Meanwhile, the parents at dinner on the West Coast will probably share more mixed perspectives. The research shows a split almost right down the middle. About half are saying, "I think *we* are responsible." The other half are saying, "You know, I think *the church* is responsible." There's dialogue happening here with questions being asked and differences expressed.

To be honest, if I could choose one of the two gatherings, I'd rather be at the dinner party on the West Coast. Why? *Dialogue over declaration.*

What we would gain from the group of ten kids' pastors is nothing we haven't heard before. It's the declaration of "Parents are the primary disciplers of their kids" and it's "Deuteronomy 6 says . . ." or even "I'm so frustrated that more parents are not taking up their spiritual responsibility." To be clear, these are all accurate statements and valid concerns. They are theologically, biblically, and practically truthful statements. And yet, it would appear that the answer to getting us unstuck from our stalemate is not another twenty years of "Parents are the primary" as our sole declaration. This is an important declaration that we must take with us into the future, but there seems to be more to our story.

Back at the dinner party on the West Coast, if we could be a fly on the wall, what would we hear? According to the data, we'd hear disagreement, discussion, and dialogue. One father says he feels an overwhelming sense of responsibility to disciple his own kids . . . a mother chimes in to share how insecure she feels about discipling her daughter . . . another father with a busy travel schedule backs her up and says he doesn't have the slightest idea where to begin with his son . . . a mom mentions how she feels so much shame from decisions in her own teen years, and besides, no one has ever *showed her* how to disciple her own kids . . . a wise grandmother pushes back gently and reverses the tide by advocating for how we at least need to *try* and take responsibility; after all, we have more available hours in a week to influence kids than they could ever get in even the best local church children's ministry.

Now this is some good dialogue! And it's this sort of dialogue we need to be facilitating (if we are not already), for it's in the middle of this disagreement, discussion, and dialogue that sparks are flying. The sparks from the friction of the push-and-pull and back-and-forth dialogue are where we discover empathy, pain points, new ideas, insight, and innovation that can lead to community transformation.

For years, church leaders have sensed that kids' pastors and parents do not agree on the domain of faith formation, and now the latest data from Barna Group helps us see more clearly that we need to get *unstuck* from our stalemate.

If you are a church leader who is feeling the pain of parents who do not engage in discipling their children at home, you are justified in your pain and frustration. It's something worth grieving. But we must go beyond our frustration and grief as church leaders and ask *new* questions. It is true that parents *should* be discipling their own kids at home. But as leaders and shepherds, we have to go beyond the "shoulds" and discover how to break the real barriers to discipleship. What if there was something church leaders *could* do differently to help get us unstuck? What if we have a role to play in why we are stuck?

As we move into the next section, we are going to evaluate how our actions can sometimes be incongruent with our thinking and our message. It is good that church leaders have championed the message "Parents are the primary spiritual influence on their kids." But do our actions support this? Why do parents seem to lack the confidence to engage their children spiritually? Have we adequately trained parents to disciple their children at home?

What if there was something church leaders *could* do differently to help get us unstuck?

We seem to be experiencing a gap in our orthopraxy. Let's next take a look at the gap between what we say and what we do.

There's a Gap in Our Orthopraxy

For those for whom the word "orthopraxy" is new or unfamiliar, here's a simple way to understand it: In a faith context, orthopraxy is the practice or actions of our theology in everyday life. It is the heart, hands, and feet of orthodoxy, the outward living of our inward belief.

One of the chief struggles with being human is this very topic. What we think and believe doesn't always translate into our actions. We see this in our own lives with food, exercise, entertainment, social media, finances, parenting, and a long list of moral issues big and small. The apostle Paul summed up this human struggle so well when he wrote, "I do not understand what I do. For what I want to do I do not do, but what I hate I do" (Rom. 7:15 NIV).

Thinking back to that popularized phrase, "Parents are the primary spiritual influence on their kids," this is a belief and a conviction. It is God-given in the Scriptures, therefore theological in nature (Deut.

6:4–9; Matt. 18:6; Prov. 22:6; Ps. 78:4–6). And it's not only biblical, but it's also communal and mathematical—it's a conversation about relational proximity and numbers. Meaning, parents have scores of hours available each year to influence their own children and the opportunity for consistent relational closeness. Church leaders, pastors, and church volunteers, on the other hand, do not have this distinct advantage in practicality.

So, as church leaders, our position of *parents are the primary disciplers of their children* is theological, biblical, *and* practical. But we still have a problem. The problem isn't with our theology, our belief, or our convictions—it's with our orthopraxy (our practices).

As a part of my leadership role, I travel quite a bit around the US as well as internationally. A high percentage of my travel is meeting with church leaders, lead pastors, and kids' pastors. In the years leading up to COVID-19, this gap in our orthopraxy became clearer in my understanding of the church-and-home stalemate. While on a tour of meetings with several churches in 2019, I was talking to Tiffany, a kids' ministry director out west. Tiffany had mentioned several times her belief and conviction that parents are primarily responsible for the discipleship of their own children. She mentioned it so frequently in this discussion, I could tell there was a lot of pain and frustration behind her passionate position. I began to gently ask questions about why she thought more parents were not stepping up and engaging. I'll never forget her response. "The most fruitful and effective way to do children's ministry is when we get relational time with parents and volunteers. They are the ones on the front lines with kids!" she said with a passion rising in her voice. "When parents are trained and equipped, discipleship with kids tends to happen more naturally and effectively."

We chatted a bit more. I was curious about her most recent comment because I thought she was hitting on the linchpin. So, I gently asked another question: How much of her (and her team's) time is spent weekly in relational time with parents? Tiffany's eyes immediately flooded with tears. She kept her composure, but the pain was palpable. She quietly yet clearly responded, "There's just so many things I'm juggling. It's unfortunate that the thing that is most influential in discipling kids is what my team does the least."

 Our actions as church leaders, kids' pastors, and pastors often do not match our firmly held belief and conviction. We believe down to our bones that parents and volunteers have tremendous relational influence over the spiritual lives of children. And we believe that the most fruitful use of our time as ministers of the gospel is to train and equip those on the front lines with kids (namely parents, caregivers, and volunteers). Yet, much like Tiffany, the latest research shows that relational investments in training parents receives the smallest portion of our time.

There's a gap in our orthopraxy.

We are not only deeply convicted that parents are primarily responsible for the discipleship of their own children, we also know from experience that the most fruitful way to help parents disciple their children is to invest in loving, caring adults relationally. Yet, we struggle in our current model of ministry (the old map) to have time to do what we know is most influential. The result? Partnering with parents seems more like an idea, and less of a reality.

As we've researched this gap in our orthopraxy, it led us to commission an entire 2022 research project on our most critical non-renewable resource: *time*. In this project we began by asking the question, "How do children's ministry leaders spend their time?" Let's take a look at what we discovered.

How Do Children's Ministry Leaders Spend Their Time?

Are you familiar with the term "behavioral baseline"? If not, and if you are willing to give yourself an hour, go check out *The Behavioral Panel* on YouTube. These guys are behavioral analysis experts who have worked with the FBI, the CIA, the US military, celebrities, criminals, global leaders, and some global leaders who are also criminals. True story. What these guys do is study facial expressions, gestures, use of language and tone, and a whole host of body language indicators to try to assess truthfulness . . . or deception.

Establishing a behavioral baseline is important for a behavioral analysis so that they can understand how a person acts when they are relaxed. If they were studying you, they'd be looking for your *behavioral reality*—just you being you. Once they have that understanding, they can compare how you behave and act when you are under stress to your baseline behavior, to determine if you are being truthful, or deceptive. It's fascinating stuff!

So, what's so important about baseline behavior? And what does that have to do with child discipleship?

Knowing how much prominence the children and family ministry community has given to the message "Parents are the primary spiritual influence on their children" (remember the 95 percent?), it's only wise for us to pause to evaluate this: Do the time investments of church leaders match our stated priorities? Meaning, if we expect parents to disciple their kids, have we trained them? But before we dive way down into how much time we spend relationally investing in parents, we first needed to establish our behavioral baseline. So in 2022, we commissioned a study titled *How Do Children's Ministry Leaders Spend Their Time?*

Our hypothesis going into the research was that relational training and equipping of parents and volunteers are what the children's ministry community says are the most fruitful ways to influence the discipling of children (investing relationally in adults who have more time with children). So, if that's the case, how much time do we spend doing those types of activities? To clarify, not how much time do you *wish* we were spending doing these things . . . simply, how often are we doing relational mentoring and training with parents? And the best way to discover and understand that is to start with our behavioral baseline. Define our reality. See how we spend our time each week. So, in this 2022 research project, we asked, "As a children's ministry leader in your church, how do you spend your time each week? Please list the top items that fill up the majority of your calendar each week."[8]

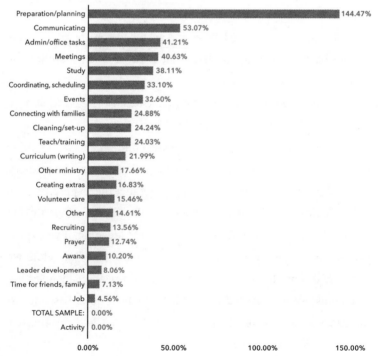

Open-end responses coded into categories 1st mention: 555; 2nd mention: 551; 3rd mention: 532; 4th mention: 467; 5th mention: 385

Notice in this open-ended question that we gave the respondents up to five opportunities to respond. The 5by5 Research Agency then went through each of the mentions and coded them based on the meaning of the response. Right away what we observe here is that there was a clear top response of Preparation or Planning, scoring a whopping 144.47 percent. How can that be? That's because each person (remember, multiple mentions) mentioned "preparation or planning" about 1.44 times on average. But wait, there's more.

#2. Communicating—53.07 percent

#3. Admin / Office Tasks—41.21 percent

#4. Meetings—40.63 percent

#6. Coordinating / Scheduling—32.60 percent

To help us understand our behavioral baseline in terms of "time spent," children's ministry leaders spend the vast majority of our time doing administrative work that involves preparing, planning, coordinating, scheduling, office tasks, communication, and meetings.

Let's be clear that those kinds of tasks aren't bad, per se. In Luke 14:28, Jesus Himself gives a nod to administrative and planning work when He says, "For which of you, desiring to build a tower, does not first sit down and count the cost, whether he has enough to complete it?" In Acts 6, we observe a division of labor between those who will serve widows through food distribution (administrative tasks) and those who are dedicated to prayer and the teaching of the Word.[9]

Without planning, our gatherings would be a train wreck. Without communication, there is no clarity. A children's ministry leader's administrative work involves important tasks, and this work must continue.

That said, the question in front of us is one of wisdom and

stewardship. I'm not questioning whether our time should be used for administrative purposes (nor do I hear anyone else questioning that). As noted above, planning and preparation are essential to facilitate our ministries and organizations. As organisms grow, organization is a must![10]

What I am questioning, and what we all need to question, is the dominance that administrative tasks have as they take over *nearly every hour* of our calendar.

So, in terms of "How does a local church children's ministry leader spend his or her time?" it's overwhelmingly clear. Our behavioral baseline is that we spend our time doing administrative tasks. It's our default. Our norm. It's the outgrowth of the old map of children's ministry. And, as a community, this is causing us a lot of consternation and grief, because we do not believe this is the most impactful use of our time.

Well, what *do* we believe is the best use of our time? Let's take a look at the next five charts from this same research study. For those of you who love data and numbers, the following will be a treat. For those who aren't crazy about data, we'd ask that you don't overlook the next section; there are treasures to be found. Be sure to take a moment to read through the data and to process the meaning and insights at the bottom of each page.

The Biggest Areas of Ministry Impact
Get the Least of Our Time

In this same 2022 study, we asked, "Regardless of how you spend the majority of your time, what are you doing that you believe will have the most impact on child discipleship?"[11]

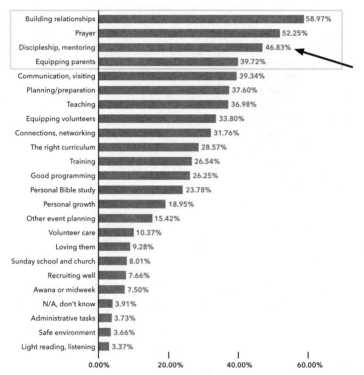

Open-end responses coded into categories 1st mention: 555; 2nd mention: 516; 3rd mention: 457; 4th mention: 325; 5th mention: 229

Forming Faith Insight: Children's Ministry Leaders believe that relational ministry investments will have the biggest ministry impact (notice: eight of the top ten are relational in nature).

This is what we really wish we could do:[12]

We asked children's ministry leaders, "What do you wish you could do (that you are not currently doing) in any of the areas in this survey to be more effective in discipling children?

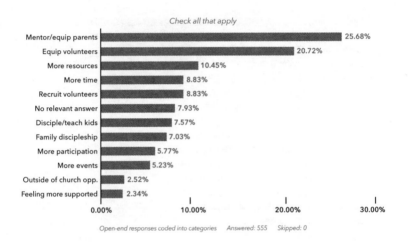

Open-end responses coded into categories   Answered: 555   Skipped: 0

Forming Faith Insight: Relationally mentoring parents and training volunteers is what we (children's ministry leaders) long to do more of to increase our child discipleship impact.

Yet mentoring, training, and discipling parents falls near the bottom of our weekly priorities. We asked children's ministry leaders, "Of the activities listed below, which ones would you say take up the majority of your time and capacity throughout a typical week?"[13]

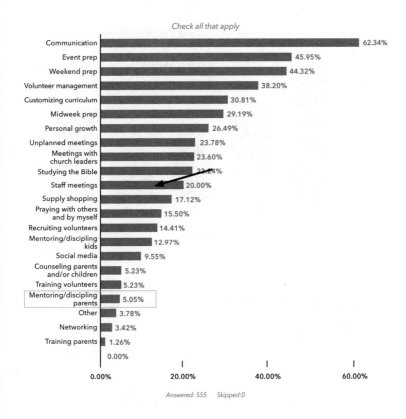

Check all that apply

Activity	Percentage
Communication	62.34%
Event prep	45.95%
Weekend prep	44.32%
Volunteer management	38.20%
Customizing curriculum	30.81%
Midweek prep	29.19%
Personal growth	26.49%
Unplanned meetings	23.78%
Meetings with church leaders	23.60%
Studying the Bible	23.24%
Staff meetings	20.00%
Supply shopping	17.12%
Praying with others and by myself	15.50%
Recruiting volunteers	14.41%
Mentoring/discipling kids	12.97%
Social media	9.55%
Counseling parents and/or children	5.23%
Training volunteers	5.23%
Mentoring/discipling parents	5.05%
Other	3.78%
Networking	3.42%
Training parents	1.26%
	0.00%

Answered: 555   Skipped: 0

Forming Faith Insight: Despite the fact that relationally investing in parents is one of the most strategic and impactful investments of our time, it simply falls near the bottom of our weekly list.

Only one-third of children's ministry leaders equip parents weekly, and over half of this group only spends one to three hours a week doing so. In this same 2022 study, we asked: "How frequently are you focusing specifically on equipping parents to help them disciple their children in any way?"[14]

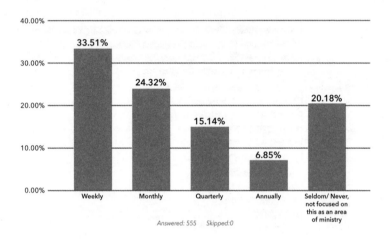

Answered: 555   Skipped:0

To amplify the results a bit:

- 33.51 percent of children's ministries invest in weekly equipping with parents (the highest performers among us).

- Of those, 56.45 percent are only spending 1–3 hours per week doing so.

- 66.49 percent of children's ministries are spending time on equipping parents on a much less frequent basis monthly, quarterly, annually, or seldom/not at all.

Forming Faith Insight: Churches that are successful at discipling kids will figure out how to incrementally prioritize increased time in their weekly and monthly calendar to relationally invest in training and equipping parents.

When churches say "equip parents," their leading strategy is actually "distributing resources." In this same 2022 study, we were trying to understand, "Specifically, what are you doing to equip parents to help them disciple their children?"[15]

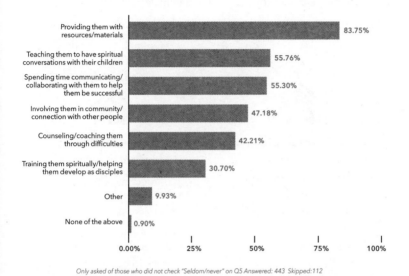

Only asked of those who did not check "Seldom/never" on Q5 Answered: 443 Skipped:112

Forming Faith Insight: Resources are helpful. However, relational training is the catalyst for higher levels of engagement of the resources.

Stalemate Summarized

The value of research is being able to employ data and information to gain wisdom and insight. Then, to be able to take that insight in order to influence gospel transformation . . . a better future . . . a future that aligns today's reality to the biblical vision of discipleship.

So, how can we move from the insights in this chapter to transformation? How can we get our agents of formation, the church and home, unstuck?

What this research illustrates is that *both* the church and the home have responsibility in why we are stuck in a stalemate. The story is not, "Parents are the primary . . . and they are not doing their job. Period." To declare that most parents are not engaging in discipling their own children is to only acknowledge half of the stalemate. Here's the summary of what the data is revealing about both our theology *and* our orthopraxy:

Church Responsibility:
It's the role of the church to equip the saints for the work of discipleship. Church leaders are the most trained, experienced, and skilled to disciple children, yet they have the least amount of access to children.

Home Responsibility:
Parents are the primary disciplers of their kids at home. Parents have the most access to children, yet lack the confidence and experience to engage in child discipleship.

Church Reality:
Children's ministries spend most of their time on administrative work and spend very little time doing relational mentoring, training, and equipping, which church leaders believe is what will have the biggest impact on children actually being discipled.

Home Reality:
Only a small percentage of parents actively disciple their children at home. A higher percentage of parents lack confidence to disciple their children and claim they've never been trained in how to disciple their children.

The Crux of Our Stalemate

Those who are most experienced and skilled (church leaders) to train and equip parents are in a church model (the old map) that leaves little (if any) weekly time to do the work of training and equipping the saints (parents and caregivers) for the work of child discipleship. Therefore, parents are not getting trained. They lack the confidence to disciple their children, and child discipleship is simply not happening in most Christian homes. We are gridlocked.

This is the crux of our stalemate. The old map of children's ministry was designed in such a way as to perpetuate the stalemate. This is why we are stuck. If we stay in the old map, it's only rational that we should expect the same results in our highly secularized, post-Christian culture.

You are one of the pioneers of the future, drafting the new map (actually, an ancient map). It starts here, and we start together.

But there's good news! Hopeful news, actually: we don't have to stay stuck in a stalemate. There's a new map to be drawn—a fresh and healthy perspective. You are one of the pioneers of the future, drafting the new map (actually, an ancient map). It starts here, and we start together.

Dialogue Brings Perspective to Our Declaration

We have to move *beyond* the declaration of "Parents are the primary . . ." It's accurate, but incomplete. We need to take the message of "Parents are the primary . . ." with us into the future, but there's more to the story. There's another perspective. We must move from declaration (Parents are responsible!) to dialogue (Let's figure this out together). We know this biblically, and we know this from the research: parents need to be trained and equipped relationally.

But how?

Much like the stalemate negotiations throughout history, it will require that one party take on the role of leader in going from here (stalemate) to there (God's agents of formation in a thriving partnership). So, who is the leader in getting us out of the stalemate? Parents or pastors?

The Bible gives us a beautiful picture when describing the role of the shepherd and his sheep. The sheep know the voice of the shepherd (John 10:3). The shepherd pursues his lost sheep and rejoices when he finds one (Luke 15:3–7). What do we know about sheep? We know that sheep take a lot of work! When a sheep gets its hoof stuck in between the rocks, it's the shepherd who safely removes it. When a sheep is fallen and injured, it's the shepherd who carries the sheep back to safety. Acts 20:28 says, "Pay careful attention to yourselves and to all the flock, in which the Holy Spirit has made you overseers, to care for the church of God, which he obtained with his own blood." Simply stated, when the sheep are lost, the shepherd has to go and get them to guide them back to green pastures and still waters.

Church leader, this is you. Pastor, this is you. Children's pastor . . . you guessed it, this is you. And, if you are in a smaller church context, it may be you, mom or dad or volunteer leader. Regardless of the context, the sheep simply lack the vision, confidence, and experience and will not lead us out of this stalemate. And simply "declaring" the sheep to move will not get the job done. We must lead them. We must guide them. We must walk alongside them. We must shepherd them. God has called you to shepherd. To equip the saints for the work of the ministry. To go and make disciples.

Using the Bible, the latest research, and a combined seventy-five years of ministry experience, Sam, Mike, and I have put together a blueprint to equip you as a shepherd and a leader for getting us unstuck from our stalemate. We call it the Church Leader's Forming Faith Pathway.

THE CHURCH LEADER'S
FORMING FAITH PATHWAY

How can church leaders build a church model and culture that trains and equips parents to disciple their kids?

How can church leaders train and mobilize parents to cultivate a culture of discipleship at home?

 The Formational Church	Central Formational Objectives	The Formational Home
The What & Why		The What & Why
What: Consistently influence and mobilize others to champion the value of child discipleship.	**Vision:** Discipleship Drives Direction	**What:** Partner with parents to cultivate a desire for children with lasting faith in Christ.
Why: The church that understands the importance of child discipleship must be ruthlessly focused on the urgency of lasting faith, rather than the immediacy of administrative needs.		**Why:** The home that prioritizes lifelong faith in Jesus will intentionally commit to the long-term faith formation of their children over the short-term benefits of lesser value.

	Time & Place: Discipleship Is Deliberate	
What: Deliberately focus your time, team, and space so that you can formally and organically invest relationally in the training and equipping of parents.		**What:** Inspire and equip families, in light of the gospel, to spend their time and use their space counterculturally.
Why: The church that understands that time is limited will make the most of every occasion as they gather to teach and train families to disciple their children.		**Why:** The home that prioritizes lifelong faith in Jesus will organically and intentionally arrange their rhythms to consistently engage in discipling their kids.
What: Regularly clarify child discipleship in your church's shared language.	Language: Discipleship as Dialogue	**What:** Model for parents how to integrate dynamic conversations in the home in a way that speaks to the presence of Jesus in their everyday lives.
Why: Discipleship-driven churches understand that language is the means by which priorities are defined, values are assigned, and practices are designed.		**Why:** The home that leverages the power of conversation to foster faith in Jesus understands that dialogue is foundational for child discipleship.

Cultivate an intergenerational *community*.	Community: Discipleship Takes a Team	Build a "home team" of other *loving, caring adults*.
What: Cultivate an intergenerational church community where each child is seen, known, and loved by multiple caring adults. **Why:** Churches that value an intergenerational community where kids feel a sense of belonging are more fruitful in forming lasting faith in children.		**What:** Impress upon parents the value in a team of intentional relationships for the discipleship of every child. **Why:** The home that builds a discipleship team around each child creates multiple connection points that form a foundation of Christian faith.

Shared Formational Outcome:
a child with lasting, resilient faith in Jesus Christ

Notice in the Church Leader's Forming Faith Pathway there is a central spine running down the middle, joined by a left and right side. The left side of the spine is titled "The Formational Church" and the right side is titled "The Formational Home." Both sides are the responsibility of the church leader. Both sides are how the church leader can best lead, shepherd, influence, and equip the home to disciple children.

In the next two chapters, Sam and Mike are going to walk through the blueprint in detail, covering how to shape both the Formational Church and the Formational Home.

As you navigate through these chapters, you will get equipped with a fresh perspective and strategy for doing child discipleship, family ministry, and children's ministry in *today's* world. Away with outdated maps that were built for decades past and on to a new map that's built for today's child, in today's world, and today's church (built on the ancient foundation). You'll be challenged to think differently about how we do children's ministry, with the motivation of becoming more effective at forming child disciples in our new realities. In addition, you'll have a clear understanding of how to lead and guide today's parents as you train and equip them to take steps forward to disciple their own children.

The turn of this page is one small action in the grand scheme of your life. Yet, pressing forward to the next two chapters could change the trajectory of your church community and countless children who will lead the future of the church.

But before we turn this page, let's go back to that imaginary dinner party on the West Coast. Remember how the parents were struggling as they processed through their thoughts?

A mother chimes in to share how insecure she feels about discipling her daughter . . . another father with a busy travel schedule backs her up and says he doesn't have the slightest idea where to begin with his son . . . a mom mentions how she feels so much shame from decisions from her teen years, and besides, no one has ever *showed her how* to disciple her own kids.

This may be an imaginary scenario. But it's not imaginary to many of the parents in your church community. It's quite real. They *do* feel insecure. Many of them don't have the slightest idea where to begin. And they feel shame from their past that prevents them from engaging in discipling their own kids.

We have such hope in Christ Jesus. And we have hope in discipling the next generation. We don't have to stay stuck in our stalemate. Let's continue to declare the unchanging truths of Deuteronomy 6:4–7, but let's not stop there. Let's learn from the insight of a fresh perspective and move from that declaration into dialogue. God has called you to shepherd: to relationally equip parents. To equip the saints for the work of ministry. To go and make disciples. Let's press on to the Formational Church.

QUESTIONS FOR REFLECTION

1. If you were to plot the parents in your church into the following segments (as it relates to discipling their own children) by percentage, what would that look like?

    ___ Highly engaged

    ___ Occasionally engaged

    ___ Rarely engaged

    ___ Never engaged

2. What would you say each of these groups of parents needs from you as a pastor, shepherd, or leader to take steps toward increased engagement in discipling their own children?

3. Consider looking at your weekly calendar from a three-month view. What patterns do you notice? What are the different ways or categories of how you spend your time? What do you tend to spend the majority of your time doing?

4. What's the one thing you wish you could do that you think would help you, your church, or parents to become more effective at discipling children?

CHAPTER SEVEN

Gaining Perspective

- Does your church have a distinct and clear vision for child discipleship?

- What are two activities you are not presently doing that you can promote and advocate for child discipleship at your church? Be specific.

- What stories can you share today with a peer or parent that illustrate discipleship or life change in the children in your church?

• • •

CHAPTER SEVEN

The Formational Church

---+---

SAM: Space has been named the final frontier. We live in a world that has significantly benefited from the scientific revolution. We understand how earthquakes happen, and what dinosaurs probably looked like, and we have discovered and named most species on our planet. We have explored every nook from the North Pole to the South Pole. Space is more understood than ever before and equally as mysterious as it's ever been.

Growing up in the 1980s, space was a big deal. Every kid wanted to be an astronaut. We turned every cardboard box into a rocket. Our grandparents pretended to be cowboys from the Old West. We dreamed of being astronauts in space.

I remember the morning of January 28, 1986, like it was yesterday. We walked into class on that frigid midwinter day like we did any other day. There was a TV in the front of the room strapped to a media cart. We asked our teacher if we were going to watch a movie. He explained that we were going to watch the first citizen, who also happened to be the first teacher-astronaut, be launched into space.

We were filled with excitement and wonder. We were thrilled to be missing work and eager to see a rocket launch live in real time.

We quickly found our seats, and the anticipation built all morning. Around 9:30 a.m. (CST), we turned on the TV and watched as experts talked about what the crew would be doing on their mission. As launch time neared, the excitement built. Our teacher talked about the importance of space and how this was such a historic moment.

As we reached ten seconds to launch, our class counted down together until blastoff. Once the engines ignited and launched, we cheered as the Challenger roared into space.

Seventy-three seconds later, we stared in stunned disbelief as the *Challenger* broke apart on live TV. I remember the quiet of a room of sixth graders trying to process what they'd just seen. I can still see our teacher standing in the front of the room, looking at the TV with tears in his eyes. That moment for me was the first time I experienced the pain of loss, a loss of innocence, a loss of hope, and joy turned to sorrow in a moment.

We all knew that was not how that day was supposed to end.

I remember hearing many months later that something as small as an O-ring in the fuel tank that had become brittle in the cold weather of that fateful morning had failed, causing such a devastating loss. When I got older and began to read reports that were commissioned to find the issue so that we did not repeat the same thing in future flights, the reports repeatedly stated that the problem wasn't just faulty mechanics but unheeded warnings from engineers about the potential danger. NASA managers approved the launch, leading to the tragic disaster. Repeated. Unheeded. Warnings.

In the opening chapters of this book, we heard warnings telling us that what most kids believe by age thirteen, they believe for the rest of their lives. We are up against a time crunch. We see data telling us that kids are walking away from the church at alarming rates. These are warnings that we must take seriously. We cannot do ministry in the same way we have for the past thirty years when research by Barna shows that 64 percent—nearly two-thirds of our kids—are walking away from the faith. These warnings, like the unheeded warnings of NASA, will cause mass devastation.

Houston, we have a problem.

We have to move from entertainment-focused environments to ones that are deeply cultivated in relational investment. We know that the most foundational indicators of lifelong faith in kids are measured by biblical engagement and relational investment. But not just us as church leaders and volunteers at church—parents too! Yet, the church and home largely remain stuck in our stalemate.

Moving beyond the message "Parents are the primary" to actually relationally training and equipping parents to be in true partnership with the church to disciple their children together is perhaps our biggest challenge. As a pastor myself, I genuinely believe that if we don't relationally equip the saints to disciple their own children, then we may be guilty of pastoral malpractice (saying one thing, but doing another). Discipleship is relational,

Discipleship is not just a feature of our ministry; it has to be the focus of everything we do.

and it takes time and effort. Equipping the saints for the work of the ministry (especially the work of the ministry in their own homes) will require that we do things differently.

What brings me deep hope and encouragement, however, is that this is not only possible, it's the most rewarding work of the church in the gospel of Christ! Discipleship is not just a feature of our ministry; it has to be the focus of everything we do.

In this chapter, we are introducing a pathway to help you actually train and equip parents to engage in the discipleship of their own children—the Church Leader's Forming Faith Pathway that Matt introduced at the end of chapter 6. As a children's ministry leader, youth ministry leader, or pastor, as we look at the four Central Formational Objectives, it's our job to ask this key question as we think about how to maximize the impact of our local church ministries: How can church leaders build a model and a culture that trains and equips parents to disciple their kids?

We don't want parents to continue to live in the frustration of feeling insecure (like they can't do this) or unequipped (like they don't know how). Therefore, we must move beyond simply telling parents to disciple their kids to actually showing them how. This is precisely the question we will address in this chapter.

Start with the End in Mind (Prior to Launch??)

If we want our churches to be the leading force in the necessary partnership of parents and the church, we have to start with a goal in mind. A picture of what success looks like. We need clarity, and we need a goal. If we don't know what we want or what a disciple looks like, we may say a lot of good things, but our vision will not be clear or compelling if we don't know what we are trying to accomplish.

John F. Kennedy, in his famous speech at Rice University, said, "We choose to go to the moon. We choose to go to the moon in this decade and do the other things, not because they are easy, but because they are hard, because that goal will serve to organize and measure the best of our energies and skills, because that challenge is one that we are willing to accept, one we are unwilling to postpone, and one which we intend to win."[1]

Kennedy was specific, he was clear, and his goal was measurable. This kind of vision-focused leadership is needed in our churches and homes more than ever. Most churches want their kids to love and follow Jesus. Fewer churches have an idea of what that looks like and how to achieve it.

I remember hearing a story of a farmer who had targets painted on the side of his barn, and every target had a bullet hole, and every bullet hole was a bull's-eye. A neighbor was impressed with the skill of the farmer. To hit that many bull's-eyes was the sign of a true marksman. He asked the farmer how he had learned to be so gifted. The farmer said, "What bull's-eyes?" The confused neighbor pointed to all of the bull's-eye targets on the side of the barn. The farmer laughed and said, "Oh, I just shoot at my barn and paint the targets over the bullet holes."

This is what we do when we focus on attendance and engagement with events and activities as our goals. The modern church (and the Western church in particular) shoots at the side of the barn and then paints bull's-eyes, saying that because our programs are full, we are successful. I don't say this as an outside critic but as a pastor and a church leader myself. I did this, and most of us have operated this way. We think, *Because people are coming, they're being discipled.* Yet we *know* that attendance does not equal Christlikeness.

As Eugene Peterson wrote, "There is a great market for religious experience in our world; there is little enthusiasm for the patient acquisition of virtue, little inclination to sign up for a long apprenticeship in what earlier generations of Christians called holiness."[2]

What Peterson observed is an epidemic in the church. We crave experiences that are little more than scattershot on the side of the barn with targets drawn after. We don't like the patient acquisition of virtue, much like learning how to fire a gun in such a way that we hit every target we aim at. We need a clear, concise, measurable picture of what a fully discipled follower of Christ looks like.

We live in a fast and shallow culture that is antithetical to the slow and deep work that discipleship entails. To be faithful to Christ's last command, discipleship needs to drive the direction of our ministries in the deliberate ways we model our faith and communicate what matters most.

As church leaders and lay leaders within our church communities, this is the culture in which we lead, serve, influence, and navigate. And we are gridlocked. But we know we can't stay stuck in a stalemate. It's our job to shepherd and lead. So, in this chapter, we will answer the question,

> As a leader or lay leader, what is my responsibility
> to help my church become a *formational* church
> to break through the church-and-home stalemate?

Using the Forming Faith Pathway as our guide, let's get started with *Vision*.

Vision: Discipleship Drives Direction

Before we walk down a pathway, we want to be sure of where it is taking us. Likewise, before we start talking about a compelling vision, before we drive the direction of our efforts, we must be sure of where we are headed. In the previous section we discussed the importance of a common goal, a common idea of what a fully developed disciple should look like. In this section we will explore the first of four stops along the Forming Faith Pathway. The faith formation of the next generation doesn't happen by accident; it is the result of the Holy Spirit's work and our effort, and it starts with a church painting a compelling vision of lifelong faith.

So, as leaders in our church community, how do we influence the vision for child discipleship? It begins with a clear understanding of the *what* and the *why*.

What: Consistently influence and mobilize others to champion the value of child discipleship.

Why: The church that understands the importance of child discipleship ruthlessly focuses on the urgency of lasting faith, rather than being dominated by the immediacy of administrative needs.

We live in a culture that is obsessed with identity, which can be a good thing. The problem is to whom or to what we attach our identity. So often, we gravitate to what is temporal and transient. "We are disciples first and parents, employees, pastors, deacons, and spouses second. Disciple is an identity; everything else is a role. Our roles are temporary but our identity will last forever."[3]

Discipleship is more than a set of beliefs that we aspire to; it's an identity that marks who we are. It is more than a cold transfer of information. Discipleship is a daily practice of death to self, a daily losing ourselves in our Beloved. The direction our churches can so often settle for is the subtle measurements of attendance, giving, and devotional activity. Those are all by-products of a follower of Christ, but by themselves they are targets drawn on the side of the barn. They are bull's-eyes that miss the mark.

So, how do you, as the champion of this compelling vision of discipleship, make this a practical reality in your church?

Think Decades, Not Days

Discipleship is and should be our most urgent priority. Yet we must never mistake urgency for expediency. Just because something is urgent doesn't mean that it is quick or easy. In our microwave, Instant Pot, and Instagram culture, we live for the ever-elusive *now*. We often do this at the expense of the past and without regard to the future. Our culture is so consumed by what is in front of us that we can't give ourselves to what we know and to what we say matters most. In the study we looked at earlier by Awana and the 5by5 Research Agency, kids' ministry leaders were asked to state what is the most important thing they do. The vast majority got it right—discipleship and prayer. When asked what they actually do, we see how the immediacy of meetings and administrative tasks swallowed up the time and energy required to do what we know is of first importance.

All discipleship is slow and subtle in so many ways, but kids' ministry is even more so. If you want to see the fruit of a life given to discipleship, especially the discipleship of kids, you have to think decades, not days.

I remember going to see a famous evangelist as a kid with my grandpa. At the end when the evangelist gave a call for salvation, thousands of people flooded the area in front of the stage. That was immediate, but it wasn't discipleship. Those pictures of mass evangelism have so permeated our national consciousness that we think anything less than a flooded altar is a failure. The slowness of ordinary obedience is painful, and discipleship is not flashy. It is not instant; it's the constant application of truth and grace over the course of years and decades.

One of the things that used to bother me as a children's pastor was that every kid I spent time with and personally discipled, when they graduated, would thank the *youth* pastor for the influence they'd had in their life. I struggled because it seemed like my life, my efforts, and my words had little lasting impact on the lives of the kids I was called to serve. It looked as if they had forgotten it. God had to remind me that He does His best work in slow, simple, ordinary obedience over time. I trust Him because His Word is true. Over time, when they were starting to have families of their own, many former students reached out and thanked me for investing in their lives when they were kids.

In Galatians 6, Paul encouraged his flock to think exactly in this way. He addressed the need for true teachers who love the truth and love God's people. He writes, "And let us not grow weary of doing good, for in due season we will reap, if we do not give up" (Gal. 6:9). Sustained work with little visible results will most often produce disappointment and discouragement. Paul was saying to us to teach, do good, but think years and decades, not days and months. This is both a rebuke and an encouragement for parents and leaders who are looking for fast, easy, and simple.

Consistent faithfulness over time does not mean that what we do is unimportant. Nothing could be further from the truth. In chapter 5, Mike clearly articulated we are up against a deadline. Because this is true, we need God's help to work with urgency in training parents in teaching kids, but we also have to trust God with the outcomes of our urgent, sustained faithfulness over time.

> **Disciples are formed in communities.**

Discipleship is not complicated, but neither is it easy. You can't do it alone. You need help. The oft-quoted maxim "It takes a village to raise a child" (more about that in chapter 8) is almost right. It takes a family to raise a child: a family of origin, and the family of God. It's a partnership. Disciples are formed in communities.

Measure What Matters

A disciple-driven church is marked, not measured. Our society loves things we measure. We attend our five-year-old's U8 soccer game that has no score, but when the final whistle blows, we know who won and how many goals our child scored. (The kids know too.) We are built for keeping score. In church, we want to know we are "winning," so we count things. Farmers know better: planting seeds and growing crops requires a ton of effort mixed with a ton of patience, because to make something grow, you need good soil, but once you plant and water, God does what only He can do (1 Cor. 3:6–7).

The reality is that if you ask any parent what they want for their kids, they will all say that they want them to do better and be better than the parents have. What they rarely say is to love Jesus more. The by-product of this drive is we put our kids in sports and make sure they have the rest they need at the expense of relationships in the church and of discipleship in the home.

We, as ministry leaders, must get our parents to see the value of a life lived *corem deo* (before the face of God). Every sporting event is a good gift, not a replacement for the one true God. Every academic achievement is the result of study but also of God's empowering grace.

The center of our message, the benchmark of our discipleship, is not in our technique but in our message.

Discipleship is not easy. It takes intentional parenting. We can shuttle our kids from event to event. That's easy. What is more difficult is to know the sorrows and the joys, walking with those we lead as they face challenges and sorrows, and in those seasons, pointing them to Jesus. That takes time and effort. Discipleship is not quick and doesn't make really cool Instagram posts. Discipleship is the slow, consistent application of truth over decades. It happens so slowly that no one notices until it is so obvious that everyone asks, "What happened to Bill?" or "What happened to Sue? She looks like an entirely different person."

Ministry leader, you must cast a compelling vision to your pastor and parents. One that helps them see that everything they do is before the face of God.

Gospel, Not Novel

Finally, in casting a compelling consistent vision, think gospel, not novel. The epicenter of our faith is not something new or innovative. The center of our message, the benchmark of our discipleship, is not in our technique but in our message.

Whenever someone comes to me and says they have a new revelation, red flags start flying. We love new and novel, and that may be okay as long as it is not at the expense of true and eternal.

In our discipleship strategies, we want new ideas and new approaches. What we need are old truths communicated in new ways. The heart of our discipleship is not doing whatever it takes to get people in the door to hear a fifteen-minute message. The heart of our discipleship must always be the gospel. The message of our lack and God's supply. The ability to disciple is not the result of a seminary course but of a heart gripped by the gospel and transformed by Christ.

Moses, after he reminded the people of the law in Deuteronomy 5, told them to disciple their kids and families, but first to make sure their own hearts were gripped by the law of God: "And these words that I command you today shall be on your heart" (Deut. 6:6).

You cannot give to your kids, your leaders, or your team what you are not. The commands of God and ways of God must permeate your life and have necessarily apprehended your affections. To disciple others requires you to be a disciple.

This shared vision of what counter-formative discipleship looks like is derived from Scripture, brought to the forefront of church life by pastors and leaders, and illustrated by influential families that see the value, need, and command to disciple their own kids and model what that looks like to their communities of faith. This compelling vision seen in the lives of families and leaders living it out will do more for families who are not currently proactively discipling their kids than programs or resources alone. They see the fruit of intentional, systematic, and urgent application of truth and grace over time.

This is not new. This is not novel. There is no hipster version of discipleship. The reality is everyone is being discipled by someone into something. We see it in the things our culture says we must have or must do for our life to have ultimate meaning. To be a disciple of Christ means Jesus is our goal, the gospel is our message, and His church is our passion.

To be a disciple of Christ means Jesus is our goal, the gospel is our message, and His church is our passion.

If we want to hear, "Well done, good and faithful servant" (Matt. 25:21), we must know the heart, direction, and desire of our Master.

Child discipleship is counter-formation. To cultivate a community of parents and congregants who long to be formed by God in ways that run counter to this world does not simply happen by accident. It happens among church communities through a shared North Star. It happens when shepherds and leaders are humble yet courageous enough to point the way by casting a consistent and ongoing compelling gospel vision to engage children in the most important journey ever: apprenticeship to Jesus Christ. Discipleship drives our direction, and we take others along with us on this journey when we cultivate a consistent and compelling vision for discipleship. Not only our own discipleship but the discipleship of our children.

In a culture where the immediacy of the temporal robs from the urgency of the eternal, we need senior pastors and influential parents who see the urgency of the deadline we are up against. Who see the value of the gospel being central in our practices and who finally are willing to play the long game that a long obedience in the same direction requires.

Now, let's pause to consider some of the content we've covered together so far in this chapter.

QUESTIONS FOR REFLECTION

1. How does the idea that "disciple" is an identity and everything else is a role resonate with you?

2. In your role as a pastor, parent, or leader, how can you ensure that the heart of discipleship remains centered on the gospel rather than getting caught up in novel or trendy methods?

3. In your church, what alternative or additional measurements might better reflect the impact of discipleship?

4. This section has emphasized the slow, consistent application of truth over decades for discipleship to produce lasting change. How does this perspective challenge or affirm your expectations of discipleship in your own life or in the community you're part of?

Time and Place: Discipleship Is Deliberate

Having looked at a clear and compelling vision that is understood and urgently acted on by our senior leadership and influential parents, we want to continue to focus on this question: How can church leaders build a model and a culture that trains and equips parents to disciple their kids?

We must ensure that we are leveraging the time we have with parents when we are together. This might include times for formal training and informal conversation, with the goal of encouraging, training, and developing parents so they are confident and equipped to disciple their kids. Let parents see the relationship you have with them as a true partnership in the gospel.

With this in mind, let's turn our focus to the second of four areas of the Church Leader's Forming Faith Pathway: *Time and Place.*

What: Deliberately focus your time, team, and space so that you can formally and organically invest relationally in the training and equipping of parents.

Why: The church that understands that time is limited will make the most of every occasion they gather to teach and train families to disciple their children, knowing they must reach people while everyone is gathered.

Discipleship doesn't happen on its own. Disciples don't appear because you say it's a core value on the About Us section of your website. If we approach our discipleship process like time-cooking a rotisserie chicken—set it and forget it—we will drift off course and end up years later in a place asking how we got there.

In 1492, Columbus set sail from Spain with the goal of reaching Asia by sailing westward across the Atlantic Ocean. However, due to miscalculations in his navigation, the misjudgment of the distance to Asia, and incorrect maps, Columbus and his crew ended up landing on the island of Guanahani in the Bahamas, which was nowhere near their intended destination. According to Columbus's journal, he had initially intended to reach the eastern coast of Asia, but he failed to account for the size of the Earth and the existence of the Americas. As a result, he underestimated the distance he needed to travel to reach Asia and ended up in the Caribbean instead.[4]

This is the current state of so much of our discipleship. If asked, many of us would say that discipleship is our primary objective as a church. The ways we achieve that goal are less clear. Several years ago, I was at a family ministry conference, and in every conversation, I would weave in the question, "What are you doing in your ministry to specifically create disciples of the next generation?" I got many blank stares. A few said we disciple kids in the weekend service, and a few said they provide tools like take-home papers. This is not the kind of discipleship that produces lifelong followers of Christ. Take-home papers, although potentially helpful if they are engaged by parents, are not a strategy for creating resilient followers of Christ. They are a small, too-often-overutilized tactic in a lifelong discipleship journey.

We Have to Get Them While We've Got Them

There has been a correct emphasis on parental involvement in the discipleship of kids. Hear me: nothing has the time and formative force of the influence a parent has on a child. What stats have shown (such as Barna's study on church confidence) is that we, as pastors and leaders, have lost confidence in the formative power of the church and the gospel. Parents come to church looking for guidance and wisdom. They want help, and they themselves need to be discipled. We have to leverage the time we have when parents are in the building.

This is so important for the lifeblood of our church that we must make the training and discipleship of parents a primary focus. That may look different at your church, but if your vision is compelling, your pastor will see the need and want to respond.

What do we do when our pastor says what should we do? Seize the day. Here are a few ideas to train parents while you already have them on your church campus.

- If you have more than one service, have parents attend a worship service as normal, and at the second service, do a training event to help parents understand the role they play in the life of their kids.

- Just as some churches have a "Next Steps" or "New Believers" class or a "Prepare for Baptism" experience, consider taking this same approach to training parents on how to disciple their kids. The idea is to use the model your church has for training already, but add something intentional to train parents.

- Do a Back-to-School Sunday where you interview parents on stage who are already doing the work of discipleship well.

- Have a Sunday school class where you walk through family discipleship strategies for your home.

- Host a meal. After your Sunday services, do a family lunch or dinner together and talk about how we faithfully train our kids to live before the face of God.

- On Wednesdays, when parents drop their kids off at youth ministry, have a small group for parents that helps them understand their changing role as disciples in the life of their teenagers.

These ideas are representative of endless opportunities that you have to connect with, train, and disciple parents while they are already at church or attending church-related activities. I (Sam) have found that training events are much more successful if you connect them to something parents are already attending at church—and include food. Maybe this is because my wife is Italian and food is a huge deal in our home. Or because the northeastern US is obsessed with food and, despite what Mike or Matt say, New York pizza is the *only* real pizza. But I don't think it's just that. Food was a central part of the Gospels; how often did Jesus disciple His disciples over a meal? The answer is: often.

A Word to Large Churches

I currently serve in a church that has five locations. The smallest is around eighty people, the largest about a thousand. While we are by no means one of the largest churches in America, we are bigger than many, and some of the above ideas for connecting with parents will work, but many won't because of the number of families you serve and the schedule your church maintains. For example, on a Sunday morning, I can't do a meeting for parents because we use every room in our church building.

Here are a few ideas for a larger church for connecting with parents while you have them:

1. Connect in the halls before and after service. Make sure you or senior members of your kids' ministry team are available to smile, connect, and have conversations with parents at drop-off and pick-up.

2. Consider hosting a parenting seminar on another night but with full participation and buy-in from your senior leader.

3. Talk to your senior pastor about illustrations and stories he can use in his sermons that will help reinforce the value of child discipleship.

4. Proactively spend time with your senior pastor and senior leadership team to ensure they understand the vision needed to train and equip parents to disciple their kids. First by doing this themselves, and second, by using common language together (we'll talk more about this a bit later) in communicating to the church at large and their direct spheres of influence within the church.

5. Leverage your communications teams to find ways to communicate the value of child discipleship across the campus through print, social media, and video content.

The reality is many parents don't know how to disciple their kids or see it as a lower value than they should. We need to get to parents while we have them.

To say parents are solely responsible lets the church off the hook. On the other hand, to say the church staff are the professional disciplers and they need to do it all lets the parents off the hook. We see this in church all the time; it's the stalemate that Matt described in chapter 6.

We need to realize that in the discipleship of children, it isn't the parents' responsibility, it isn't the church's responsibility—it's both. For our part, the church needs to use the time and influence we have with parents to disciple and train them to effectively disciple their kids (while realizing that not every parent is willing, trained, or even physically present).

We as the church need to leverage the time we have with kids on the weekend, during the week, and at special events where kids can have a sense of belonging, grow in their understanding and belief about who God is, and ultimately become who He created them to be.

This will not happen through finger-pointing and blame-shifting. It happens through the intentional use of the time that we have to form kids into the image of God. This is why we are so passionate about relationship-driven teaching connected to biblical engagement, because we think that is how formation and becoming happen best.

Let's take another quick pause to reflect on what we continue to learn in this chapter.

QUESTIONS FOR REFLECTION

1. How can church leaders strike a balance between formal training and informal conversations to encourage, train, and develop parents, ensuring they feel confident and equipped to disciple their children?

2. How can churches avoid drifting off course in their discipleship efforts and ensure a clear and intentional path?

3. In the context of your own church, how might the suggested ideas for training parents be adapted to create meaningful connections and discipleship opportunities, especially considering the size and structure of your church?

4. This chapter emphasizes the joint responsibility of parents and the church in the discipleship of children. Reflect on the importance of avoiding a "stalemate" situation and finding ways to collaborate effectively. How can churches foster a sense of shared responsibility without shifting blame between parents and the church?

Language: Discipleship as Dialogue

If you can change the language, you can change the culture.

Having looked at a clear and compelling vision, as well as the need to leverage our time with parents to help them see the value and urgency of child discipleship, we now turn to discipleship as dialogue, and the formative power of shared language.

What: Regularly clarify child discipleship in your church's shared language.

Why: Discipleship-driven churches understand that language is the means by which priorities are defined, values are assigned, and practices are designed.

"It Is Not Childcare. It Is Children's Ministry."

Pro tip: If you want to send a kids' pastor through the roof, call what they do *childcare*. While sometimes it might seem like it, caring for the physical well-being of a child is only part of what they do. The problem is that calling what kids' pastors do *children's ministry* may be better, but even that term is incomplete. I prefer to call what kids' pastors do *child discipleship* because it speaks to the forming of a child's body, soul, and spirit by pointing them to Christ. Discipleship is not just something adults do. It's something we are all called to do.

Our words have meaning, and they have impact—significantly more than we realize.

In 1999, NASA launched the Mars Climate Orbiter mission. However, during the journey the spacecraft went off course due to a navigational error and ultimately burned up in the Martian atmosphere. The error was traced back to a mix-up in units of measurement, with one team using the metric system and another using the imperial system. This led to the spacecraft being fired with too much force, causing it to drift off course and miss its target.

As a result of this error, NASA lost a $125 million spacecraft and valuable scientific data that could have helped further our understanding of the Martian environment. The incident highlighted the importance of clear communication and standardization of measurement units in scientific missions. As NASA administrator Daniel Goldin said at the time, "We lost Mars Climate Orbiter because we failed to recognize and correct a simple, yet fundamental, error in the development of the mission software."[5]

A multimillion-dollar ship and countless hours of effort were wasted because of a lack of clarity of terms. Words matter. Terms matter. Discipleship is dialogue. The words we use disciple us. What we call something over and over again has an effect on those who are speaking and those who are hearing.

If we want buy-in from parents, we need to define terms. We need to create a shared language around the discipleship of their kids. We want their kids to have lasting faith. We need to use language that paints a picture of what we want to achieve and how we will measure and ensure lasting faith in the next generation.

KidMin Has a Birthday

Several years ago, I was watching the Super Bowl and tweeting about it. The year was 2009. The internet was a toddler, and Twitter was an infant. Right around this time some friends and I started to tweet about how kids' ministry needed a hashtag that would make all related content on Twitter easily accessible and turn random thoughts into a streaming conversation. After some debate we came up with several options: #CM #FAMIN #KIDMIN. CM was unclear, and FAMIN was a little dark. The clear winner we all agreed on was KIDMIN. We started to push out to Twitter and our social media feeds this new hashtag #KIDMIN; it went viral, and within two years Children's Ministry had been renamed KIDMIN across the nation.

Why did this happen? Was it because my friends and I who thought it up were so brilliant or influential? No. It happened because we used the term KidMin enough that more people started saying it, and eventually the community as a whole started using it. What we say—and how we say it—matters.

We need to make a similar shift today. We must move from a mindset of caring for the physical well-being of kids or even being the "spiritual directors" of kids to one of being obsessed over the Christ-likeness of kids. That is why we need to start calling what we do by what it is. We have to move from what we do as *children's ministry* to *child discipleship*. We need to move from children's pastor or director of children's ministry to director of child discipleship or pastor of child discipleship. Not because a title matters in itself but because we tend to forget what matters most, and we need to be constantly reminded we are discipling the next generation in their most formative years. That is our goal, our mission, and Christ's command.

> We have to move from what we do as *children's ministry* to *child discipleship*.

This is already happening! Shaun McKinley, international director of children's ministries at Church of God of Prophecy, took to Facebook to reinforce to his followers that language matters. That discipleship happens through intentional actions and intentional words. Here is what Shaun said:

> Some changes are big. Other changes appear subtle but are bigger than we realize.
>
> For thirteen years, our mission has been "developing leaders, impacting kids." These four little words have accurately captured our work and the resources we've developed to serve our global network in 135 nations.
>
> Today, we announce a subtle change to our mission statement. Why the change? Because we believe the Holy Spirit has called us to clarify our mission so that we are focused and intentional. It's a mission that's biblical and reflects the command of Jesus. It reflects a challenge to bring our kids into a relationship—with God and others—to develop a lasting faith and join us in reconciling the world to Christ through the power of the Holy Spirit.

"Developing leaders, discipling kids." That's our mission. That's the challenge we've accepted.

Yes, the change is subtle. The impact will be BIG. Don't just watch us. Join us.

Together, we will raise the greatest generation of disciples the church has ever known.[6]

If you want to change the culture of the children's ministry world, you have to change its language. Because what we say and how we say it betrays what our hearts love and what we value most.

"They Are Just Kids"

The second way you can make the pastor of child discipleship angry is to say, "But they are just kids." Discipleship of kids requires us to listen and speak. Kids are not only capable of being disciples; they are, by Christ's own definition, what disciples most closely resemble.

"Who Is the Greatest?"

At that time the disciples came to Jesus, saying, "Who is the greatest in the kingdom of heaven?" And calling to him a child, he put him in the midst of them and said, "Truly, I say to you, unless you turn and become like children, you will never enter the kingdom of heaven. Whoever humbles himself like this child is the greatest in the kingdom of heaven." (Matt. 18:1–4)

The culture of Jesus's day saw children as less important, so what He said was countercultural. To our culture, which in many ways worships youth, this is likewise countercultural. Jesus was correcting His disciples, telling them that this child has infinite value. For our day, He tells us the child's value isn't in the potential of sporting, academic, or financial success. Our hope isn't in us living our second life through the lives of our kids.

Jesus is telling us moderns that the most profound thing about kids is their ability to believe in things they don't fully understand. Their humble position is utterly dependent on their parents for life. We need to drop the façade of self-reliance and cling to Christ the way a child clings to his mother.

Kids need *us* to train and form their loves and train their hearts. We need *them* to show us what radical, humble dependence looks like. The way this is accomplished is through everyday communication: listening to children as adults with real (not feigned) interest, and discipling them in everyday conversations that originate from the Word of God and the world He has made.

To be better disciples, we need to learn to listen. To be better disciplers of others, we need to know when to speak and what to say.

As the pastor of child discipleship, your influence probably does not reach as far as your lead pastor's. If you want to change the language of your parents and the culture of your church, you need your pastor to not just agree but to champion these culture-transforming initiatives.

If we want to change the culture of our churches, we have to be willing to lead. One of the best ways we can do that is to help our senior leaders use language that is infused with the values of discipleship. Your senior pastor will be the one who speaks to parents most often. Getting your senior leader to be on the same page, with a shared lexicon that reflects the values of what you are doing and why, will go a long way to helping parents see what you are doing is churchwide, not just a kids' pastor's preference.

Senior pastors want to produce disciples, of course; often they are looking to you as the child discipleship pastor for guidance as to what to say and how to say it. You need to think through what words or phrases best reflect the importance of discipleship and the need for partnership. Here are a few things you could have your pastor convey from the pulpit:

1. George Barna says that what kids believe by the time they are thirteen is what they will die believing. What our kids' team is doing and what you are doing as parents is more important than anything else. Our kids need to know that they are loved (Belong), know that the Bible is true and they can trust it (Belief), and know that God has a plan for them (Become).

2. Our church values the Word of God and the need for each child to understand the story of Scripture and how to apply it to their lives. That is why we call what we do child discipleship, not kids' ministry or childcare. Child discipleship addresses the physical, spiritual, and social well-being of our children.

3. We as a church don't look at parents as the only ones responsible for discipleship, but as partners with us in the discipleship of our church's children.

4. We call our volunteers who work with kids Child Disciplers—because our main focus needs to be the discipleship of kids and the forming of their hearts above all else.

5. Discipleship happens best in relational environments that are deeply scriptural. Both (relationships and Scripture) are necessary for us to disciple kids in the way of Jesus.

Discipleship is an activity driven by intentionality. Intentional time spent together and intentional language create a common lexicon that parents hear over and over, that discipleship isn't just a good idea or an item on a to-do list. It is the last command of Jesus and needs to be the highest priority of the church.

If we are going to transform our church communities to be places where entertainment and fun serve biblical literacy and gospel centrality, we need our parents and leaders to see the need and speak the same language. A church where parents see the value of relationship (Belong), Scripture (Believe), and counter-formation (Become) will only happen if we have a shared vision and a common language.

It's time for another brief pause to chew on some of the insights we've just covered.

QUESTIONS FOR REFLECTION

1. The section suggests that changing the language used by church leaders can contribute to transforming the culture of a church community. Reflect on ways you can strategically shape language and terminologies to align with a vision for child discipleship. How can shared terminology and language contribute to a shared understanding and commitment among parents, leaders, and the broader congregation?

2. How does this chapter's emphasis on the role of language in shaping the culture of child discipleship within a church speak to you and your ministry setting?

3. We have discussed the subtle yet impactful shift in mission from "developing leaders, impacting kids" to "developing leaders, discipling kids." Reflect on how such small changes in language can influence the focus and priorities of an organization. What are some areas in your ministry where a change in language could better convey the value and significance of child discipleship?

4. The role of senior pastors is vital in shaping language and values related to child discipleship. Consider the influence of leadership language in your own community or organization. How might aligning senior leadership with a shared lexicon positively affect the perception of child discipleship among parents and the broader congregation?

Top 10 Things Every Pastor Should Say About Kids Each Year

1. "Children are a Blessing"—Express the biblical perspective that children are a gift from God and a source of joy for families and the community.

2. "Child Discipleship"—Explain that what we do for kids in our church is not primarily entertainment-driven or moralistic lessons, but is focused on engaging, gospel-centered discipleship.

3. "Partnering with Families"—Emphasize the importance of supporting families in their role as significant spiritual influencers in a child's life, promoting a collaborative effort between the church and families.

4. "Urgency of the Eternal"—Stress that we are up against a deadline, knowing that what kids believe by age thirteen they will die believing. We must urgently seek to encourage and strengthen truth in the hearts of our kids.

5. "Intergenerational Connections"—Encourage relationships between different age groups within the church, fostering mentorship and mutual learning experiences between older and younger members.

6. "It Takes a Family to Raise a Child"—It takes more than a village to raise a child; it takes a family of origin and a family of faith.

7. "Teachable Moments"—Stress the importance of creating an environment where children can learn about God's love and teachings through meaningful and age-appropriate lessons in organic ways.

8. "The Future of the Church"—Emphasize that children represent the future of the church, and investing in their spiritual growth is an investment in the longevity and vitality of the congregation.

9. "Pray for the Next Generation"—Encourage the congregation to pray consistently for the children of the church, asking for God's guidance, protection, and blessings on their lives.

10. "Invest in the Next Generation"—Consider serving in our kids and youth ministries, leveraging the gifts you have been given to be a fellow child disciple maker.

Discipleship Takes Community

Now that we've walked along much of the Church Leader's Faith Formation Pathway, we've come to the final step. Before we start to address the idea that community is indispensable in child discipleship, we want to continue to focus on the question that has led us through this journey together: How can church leaders build a model and a culture that trains and equips parents to disciple their kids?

Having cast a clear and compelling vision, leveraged the time and space we have, and changed the way we speak about the discipleship of children, because of the urgency and importance it demands, we now move to the final area of the Church Leader's Forming Faith Pathway: *Community*.

What: Cultivate an intergenerational church community where each child is seen, known, and loved by multiple caring adults.

Why: Churches that value an intergenerational community where kids feel a sense of belonging are more fruitful in forming lasting faith in children.

Of all the theologians I have read, few have so clearly laid out the requirements of discipleship in such a profound way as Dietrich Bonhoeffer. In his powerful book *Life Together*, he illuminates the beauty of community in forming the human heart.

> Christian community means community through Jesus Christ and in Jesus Christ. There is no Christian community that is more than this, and none that is less than this. Whether it be a brief, single encounter or the daily community of many years, Christian community is solely this. We belong to one another only through and in Jesus Christ.
>
> What does that mean? It means, *first*, that a Christian needs others for the sake of Jesus Christ. It means, *second*, that a Christian comes to others only through Jesus Christ. It means, *third*, that from eternity we have been chosen in Jesus Christ, accepted in time, and united for eternity.[7]

What Bonhoeffer is saying here is powerful and can't be missed. Christ is the gate to true community. We can only enter into a community with each other through Him. Any community that exists outside of Christ is a pseudo-community that only mirrors reality. It also means that the greatest apologetic of the Christian faith is a Christ-centered community of people who shouldn't love each other but do because of Christ and for Christ. Finally, the community is a promise that is eternal. Our love for God and love for each other will continue because it is ordained by God, sustained by God, and guaranteed by God.

Discipleship is something that takes place in proximity to others, but it isn't proximity alone that forms us into the image of Christ. Bonhoeffer ends his brilliant book on discipleship by saying what makes a Christian community unique is not proximity to each other but shared proximity to Christ. "It is not the experience of Christian community, but firm and certain faith within Christian community that holds us together."[8]

Seeing our need for others is such a challenge in our day. We can so easily believe the lie that we don't need anyone. We celebrate self-made men, which is at best a lie and at worst a terrible delusion. We don't become anything in this life without the grace of God and the help of others.

Philip Slater, in his searching study of the way Americans live together, says that all of us desire and need community:

[Community is] the wish to live in trust and fraternal cooperation with one's fellows in a total and visible collective entity. It is easy to produce examples of the many ways in which Americans attempt to minimize, circumvent, or deny the interdependence upon which all human societies are based. We seek a private house, a private means of transportation, a private garden, a private laundry, self-service stores, and do-it-yourself skills of every kind. An enormous technology seems to have set itself the task of making it unnecessary for one human being ever to ask anything of another in the course of going about his daily business. . . . We seek more and more privacy and feel more alienated and lonely when we get it.[9]

Discipleship is a team sport. Some liken discipleship to a marathon because of the longevity of faith it requires. But marathons are run alone. Michael Jordan is the greatest basketball player of all time,[10] but he couldn't have won even one game if he had suited up while the rest of his team stayed home. A group of well-coached middle school boys working together could've beaten Michael Jordan by himself in his prime.

This means we need a multigenerational team of individuals who obsess over the Christlikeness of the kids in our church. For some of you from a smaller church that has many older members, you need to recruit and train some college-age kids and some newly married couples in their twenties. For churches that seem to attract a younger crowd, you need to intentionally reach out to some grandparents to get involved. Kids need the excitement young people bring, but they need the assurance of the seasoned crowd who has seen everything this world has to offer and yet find Jesus sweeter still.

Our kids cannot become like Christ camped in their room, reading through the Bible each year. Don't misunderstand what I am saying. If you are a disciple, you will read the Bible, but if you do not do what the Bible commands, the love of God is not in you. Community is not an option we choose or ignore. Community can only be understood through the work of Christ that draws us to one another (Eph. 2:13). We need each other. We need to see Jesus *in* one another's eyes, and we need to see Jesus *through* one another's eyes.

Discipleship does not happen only at home or at church but in partnership—the community at home and the community of church partnering together to cultivate faith and interdependence. The family is foundational to the discipleship of the child, and the church is indispensable to the discipleship of the child. Discipleship is what we are called to do.

Let's look at it this way: For parents to entirely outsource discipleship to the church is parental negligence. For us as ministry leaders to champion the message "Parents are the primary," but to not equip them, is more than a misguided notion. It is pastoral malpractice.

We have to move from a model where "parents are primary" to a model where "parents are partners," part of the community of faith that holds us together in our shared love for God and, as a result of that love, a genuine love for each other.

In summary, child discipleship must be done in the community of a family. It must happen in the home *and* in the church family. But getting parents, volunteers, and members of the community to engage in the most important work on the planet is challenging. How do we mobilize them? By working on the Church Leaders Blueprint to Breaking the Stalemate:

Discipleship Drives Direction—We must cast a compelling vision. Clearly define and articulate what a fully developed disciple looks like.

Discipleship Is Deliberate—We must equip parents and disciple kids while we have them. We can't point fingers—the church at parents, or parents at the church. We must break the stalemate through intentionality in our training and relationships.

Discipleship Is Dialogue—If we change the language, we can change our church culture. What we call things and why we call them what we call them are powerful tools to reinforce the vision and refocus us on what matters most.

Discipleship Takes Community—It is not a program; it's an intergenerational effort to pass our faith to the next generation. Entertainment is not our goal. Well-attended events are not our goal. Life transformation and Christlikeness of the next generation are our goals. We must work together as parents and church communities for this to be a reality.

"Every Christian family ought to be as it were a little church, consecrated to Christ, and wholly influenced and governed by His rules."[11]

Our churches are called to train, develop, and lead in such a way that the homes of our church are like little churches. The stalemate has pushed the church and the home into a shell game of blame. Only through intentional partnership in the gospel (Phil. 1:3–6) will our churches and homes be filled with children who treasure Christ above all else.

Pastor and author John Piper describes so clearly what it looks like for our children to be fully discipled followers of Christ.

> Parents, successful parenting is more than compliant kids. It is gospel-saturated living and teaching. Show your children how Christ, crucified for our sins, and Christ, raised for our justification, and Christ, showing the Father's love, and Christ, guaranteeing the Spirit's daily help—show them how this gospel is not just something that begins the Christian life but empowers it and shapes and sustains it. Pray and love and teach your children until Christ breaks in on their hearts and becomes their Treasure.[12]

If you are a pastor or ministry leader and you are reading this, I want to fill your heart with much-needed courage for the journey. Your role in the discipleship of the kids you lead is not a supplement to the role of the parent. You are called as a leader to obsess over the Christlikeness of the kids you lead. This is what Paul did. He didn't outsource discipleship of the people that God had entrusted in his care. He obsessed over their Christlikeness: "My little children, for whom I am again in the anguish of childbirth until Christ is formed in you!" (Gal. 4:19).

One day you will give an account as an undershepherd to the great Shepherd (Heb. 13:17). You will not give account of the creativity of your hallways, or the ways in which you cheered on the parents whom you considered the primary disciplers of the kids you led. You, as the pastor, and the parents you partner with, will give account to God for the Christlikeness of our kids.

We must obsess over that.

And now, here are a few final questions to consider before we move on to chapter 8.

QUESTIONS FOR REFLECTION

1. How does Dietrich Bonhoeffer's perspective on Christian community challenge or deepen your understanding of the role of community in the discipleship of children?

2. How intentional is your church in cultivating an intergenerational community where each child is seen, known, and loved by multiple caring adults? How might this intentional approach contribute to forming lasting faith in children?

3. In the modern context described by Philip Slater, where privacy and self-sufficiency are highly valued, how do you personally overcome the challenge of recognizing and embracing the need for community, both in your personal faith journey and in children's discipleship?

4. This chapter emphasizes the importance of moving from a model where "parents are primary" to a model where "parents are partners." Reflect on the current dynamics in your church community. In what ways can your church leaders actively facilitate and support this shift, breaking the stalemate in discipleship efforts?

CHAPTER EIGHT

Gaining Perspective

- Be bold and envision the ways you wish you could equip parents in a world without limits on time, resources, and attention.

- How are you currently living out being the greatest partner with parents in the discipleship of their kids?

- What are some areas of improvement you think you'd like to make?

• • •

CHAPTER EIGHT

The Formational Home

---◇---

MIKE: As we shift from the Formational Church to the Formational Home, let's refer back to the Church Leader's Forming Faith Pathway and consider what we've defined as the Central Formational Objectives: vision, time and space, language, and community. As church leaders, these aid in answering the following key question as it relates to discipleship in the home:

> How can church leaders train and mobilize parents
> to cultivate a culture of discipleship at home?

Good question—so what's the problem? For over two decades, churches have adopted the message "Parents are the primary spiritual influence over the lives of their children," and yet so many report to us that they just can't seem to move the needle. Meaning, as much as churches have communicated this to parents, most parents struggle to disciple their own children.

As Matt shared from the research in chapter 6, the leading strategy most children's ministry leaders in the US employ to equip parents is to hand them a resource. In that same 2022 research project, we asked, "Which describes how much parents are generally using the materials and resources you provide for them to help in discipling their children?"[1]

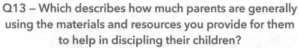

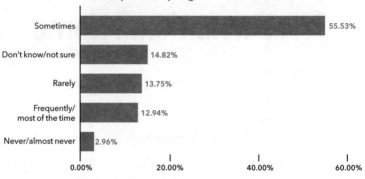

Q13 – Which describes how much parents are generally using the materials and resources you provide for them to help in discipling their children?

Only if 'providing them with resources/materials' is checked in Q11   Answered: 371   Skipped:184

As we can see, the majority of parents are only using the resources "Sometimes" (55.53 percent) by a wide margin, followed by "Don't know/not sure" (14.82 percent) and "Rarely" (13.75). Only 12.94 percent said parents are "Frequently" using the resources we provide.

Even when we feel like we put the cookies on the bottom shelf and provide materials to aid in discipleship in the home, why are so many families struggling to disciple their children? What we've discovered is that most of the children in our ministries do not live in a home that has a culture of discipleship.

You've likely heard the saying, "Culture eats strategy for breakfast." We would submit that's what's happening here. You, children's ministry leader, are working overtime trying to get parents to pray or read the Bible or have a faith conversation with their children (strategy), while most parents are living the frantic pace of life (culture).

Culture and strategy are key points of a missiological approach to missions. We often think about missiology and missions as "out there," when missionaries go to win unreached parts of the world to Jesus, thus fulfilling the Great Commission. These men and women study the people, values, practices, and history of those they intend to serve on the mission field in order to effectively make disciples, and in doing so, they create unique ways to win lost people to the Lord. However, as those committed to the mission of child discipleship, our field isn't "out there," but in the homes of the children within our communities. We need to be aware that the *strategy* of simply providing materials to aid parents in discipling their children is not going to be successful, because the *culture* of the home and society has radically changed, even in the last twenty years, and will continue to do so in this increasingly post-Christian reality. In fact, the culture, infrastructure, and systems of the average Christian household are simply not cultivating a culture of discipleship in the home.

Again, the Four Central Objectives to shape a culture of discipleship in the home are vision, time and place, language, and community. To reiterate what was covered in chapter 6, and reviewed in chapter 7, when the church and home operate in alignment in these four central formational objectives, they can shape a shared formational outcome, which is a child with lasting, resilient faith in Jesus Christ.

Let's look at the first one together.

Vision: Discipleship Drives Direction

It can be easy to throw around the word "vision" and think everyone is on the same page regarding what it means. But to better understand what we mean when we say "the vision" as it relates to equipping parents to cultivate a culture of discipleship, let's examine the *what* and the *why* of vision.

The What: Partner with parents to cultivate a desire for children with lasting faith in Christ.

The Why: The home that prioritizes lifelong faith in Jesus will intentionally commit to the long-term faith formation of their children over the short-term benefits of lesser value.

As church leaders, our vision that will allow us to break the stalemate is found when we partner with parents to cultivate a desire for children with lasting faith in Christ.

This definition of a vision or goal for discipleship becomes our *what*. But why would we commit to this? Why would we set out to do this amid the other strategies and tactics of ministry? Because we realize that the home that prioritizes lifelong faith in Jesus will intentionally commit to the long-term faith formation of their children over the short-term benefits of lesser value. There we have both the *what* and the *why* of our vision for discipleship in the home. Now let's look more closely at how this begins to take shape.

The Journey of Home Discipleship

Very rarely does one set out to drive without a destination in mind, especially with fuel prices being as high as they are. Even if you "go for a drive," you have a purpose and perhaps a destination in mind, whether it's your home at the end of the workday or a weekend-getaway spot. Rare is the person who heads off on a journey to an unknown place with no certainty of ever returning.

Running On and On and On . . .

Perhaps only Forrest Gump embarked on such a journey. For those who aren't familiar with the story and character (and without spoiling it), at one point in the book and film *Forrest Gump*, the main character, Forrest, decides to run. While recounting his life to the woman sitting next to him at a bus stop, Forrest says of this decision:

> That day, for no particular reason, I decided to go for a little run. So I ran to the end of the road. And when I got there, I thought maybe I'd run to the end of town. And when I got there, I thought maybe I'd just run across Greenbow County. And I figured, since I run this far, maybe I'd just run across the great state of Alabama. And that's what I did. I ran clear across Alabama. For no particular reason I just kept on going. I ran clear to the ocean. And when I got there, I figured, since I'd gone this far, I might as well turn around, just keep on going. When I got to another ocean, I figured, since I'd gone this far, I might as well just turn back, keep right on going.[2]

Forrest's "little run" draws media attention and curiosity. People wonder why he's running. They question his motivation. They look for a goal, a destination; they assign meaning to his effort in order to give a rationale as to why a man would just run, and run, and keep running.

This is such puzzling behavior because Forrest doesn't seem to have a direction. He's just running.

Perhaps you're a runner. I try to run most mornings, and my eldest daughter is on her school's cross-country team. Both of us run (though she's now a lot faster than I am), but we don't run aimlessly; we run for either time or distance. There is a goal in our running, as I am sure there is in your workouts. Maybe it's to be healthy (my goal), maybe to win a race (my daughter's goal), or maybe it's just to make it to a connecting flight on time at the airport (*sometimes* my goal too). Whatever the case, we typically run to achieve a goal.

In his letter to the believers in Corinth, Paul wrote: "Do you not know that in a race all the runners run, but only one receives the prize? So run that you may obtain it" (1 Cor. 9:24). Runners, outside of Forrest Gump, have a goal. In Paul's writing here to the Corinthians, he was likely referencing the biennial Isthmian Games,[3] an ancient athletic competition that took place in Corinth and was second only in size, scale, and fame to the Olympic games. The apostle Paul, in teaching the church in Corinth, used the analogy of an athletic competition, a race, to illustrate the need to be disciplined and to run toward a goal or prize. Runners run to obtain a prize; there is a goal, a destination, a very real finish line. And it's the vision of crossing the finish line that propels runners to train rigorously, to commit to eating healthy, to hydrate, to work on form and endurance, to gut it out through injury and discomfort, all in order to cross the finish line and obtain the prize.

Begin with the End in Mind

When we equip parents to develop a vision for the faith of their children, we must inspire them to start with the end in mind. For the visual thinkers among us, myself included, perhaps it's helpful to sketch out a pathway of a child's life:

Infant ····· **Child** ·········· **Teen** ····················> **Forty-year-old adult**

While any parent in the midst of raising kids will tell you the time from infant to teen seems like an eternity, what we know is that those years aren't as long as they seem, especially as we consider the timeline from teen to a forty-year-old adult. How can we help parents foster a vision that allows them to see the prize of their child walking with Jesus into adulthood? How can we help them understand that though the days are long, the years are short, and that each small moment in a child's life, each morning filled with gratitude and evening bathed in faith-filled prayer, presents a means to build faith in Jesus? We can only do so if we help parents begin with the end in mind. This is how we begin to cultivate a culture of discipleship in the home.

In his seemingly ageless work *Shepherding a Child's Heart*, Tedd Tripp asserts that we must not just begin with the end in mind, but we must develop a vision that is "clearly about man's chief end. The chief end of man is to glorify God and enjoy him forever; therefore, your objective (in speaking to parents) in every context must be to set a biblical worldview before your children."[4] For those not familiar with the language Tripp uses, it is the Westminster Shorter Catechism. Forever or eternity doesn't begin at the end of life, but at the beginning. Each parent, in thinking, dreaming, planning, and praying for who their children will become and what they will value, must have a vision that stretches into eternity but begins today. It's that vision that we need to reverse engineer from and be intentional about as it relates to rearing and raising children who will become adults with lasting faith in Jesus Christ.

Most parents' vision for their children includes academic, professional, financial, and relational goals. Ask the typical parent what they want for their child and they'll reel off no shortage of goals: straight A's, a meaningful career, a sure financial future, good friends, and a great marriage. I have never heard a parent desire their child to want less or even equal to what they themselves have, and the typical family schedule illustrates this point, but we'll talk more about that later.

One would be hard-pressed to blame a parent for desiring a great life for their child, but what does this look like as it relates to the faith of our children? If we were to talk with parents in our churches about the goals they have for their kids, would they include a lasting, thriving faith in Jesus?

Direction and Destination

Some heroes and friends of mine, Phil and Diane Comer, put it this way: "Your children will become who you tell them you see them becoming."[5]

That is the language of destination ("will become") and direction ("becoming"). Both destination and direction are essential in cultivating a vision for child discipleship. Parents must not forsake the everyday moments in light of eternity, nor need they be so focused on the day-to-day that they forget that their child will become an adult. Formation is the act of becoming, and parents can choose how intentional they will be in the formation of faith in the life of their child. Make no mistake, though: every parent is forming their child; some are just more intentional than others.

The words, actions, and attitudes of parents can and will affect the direction of their children. We, in church leadership and child discipleship, often quote Proverbs 22:6, "Train up a child in the way he should go; even when he is old he will not depart from it." Often the verse can be mistaken for a guarantee or promise, and we can feel tempted to double down on what we consider training (formal times of Bible reading, deep and involved conversations on issues of orthodoxy and orthopraxy, etc.). These are truly good and important; however, the vision parents must cultivate for their children can't just be sessions of formal training, but rather the moment-by-moment, everyday conversations where we experience Jesus and live out biblical truth in the minute-by-minute reality of life. This is the wisdom the writer of Proverbs provided.

Should we have well-thought-out times of instruction with the children in our homes? Yes! Even so, let us not forsake the moments of celebration, grief, explanation, correction, instruction, repentance, obedience, faith, forgiveness, and grace. Like driving, it is sometimes tempting to overcorrect. One family might say the best way to disciple their kids is to think "destination at all costs." This can create an attitude of legalism and a family environment devoid of grace. Another family might view their version of child discipleship as "the destination will come when it does." This can resemble grace, but it's far more like driving blindfolded. If eternity with Jesus is the destination, and eternity begins in the here and now, then the moment-by-moment, day-to-day discipleship of children is the means of direction to get to our destination. Again, destination and direction are essential in cultivating a vision for child discipleship.

Walking in the Truth

In his letter to Gaius, the apostle John writes in his greeting, "I have no greater joy than to hear that my children are walking in the truth" (3 John 4). While John isn't talking about biological children, he sets forth a vision all Christian parents can adopt for their kids: walking in the truth. In the language John uses here, inspired by the Holy Spirit, we can begin to form a picture of a vision that Christ-honoring parents can form for their children. It is that of one who is faithful to the truth of Jesus on the journey of life.

This raises a number of important questions. What does it look like for Christian parents to begin to cultivate a vision for the journey their children can walk in throughout their lives as they follow Christ? Do we, as Christian ministry leaders, speak to that vision and make lifelong faith in Jesus a goal to be obtained like we do with a child on the honor roll or in varsity athletics? Do we speak with expecting parents and work with new parents on a plan of faithfulness that will allow their children to develop lasting faith in Jesus? Are we painting a captivating picture of children growing into adults who are committed to Jesus, loving Him, and loving others well?

A Grace-Filled Aside

Let's be both honest and honoring for a moment. One of the most shame-filled experiences in the church is that of parents who feel they've done everything right, yet their child wanders away from Jesus. It can be truly difficult, even in the most loving of churches, for parents of children who have disregarded their faith. Feelings of guilt, shame, and embarrassment can flavor their experience Sunday after Sunday. We need to take a moment and acknowledge that, due to the free will we've been given as humans, there is no 100 percent money-back guarantee that faithfulness *always* produces lasting faith. However, even in the midst of God's sovereignty, we have responsibility.

We also know, from the words of Jesus, that our God is a God who seeks out those who are far from Him, that He is a Father who runs toward the prodigal with open arms, that He is rich in mercy, slow to anger, and abounding in love. These and so many more are beautiful truths about who our God is and how He is, and while they don't provide parents an excuse or an out on the responsibility to cultivate a vision for their children, they also don't condemn the parent of a child who in his or her own free will walks away from Jesus.

Helpful Questions for Parents to Consider

Before moving on to the next section, pause and think about how you might use the questions below when you are training and equipping parents to have a culture of discipleship in their own home—specifically as it relates to developing a vision for the life-long faith of their children.

- Who is the adult you see your child growing into?

- Imagine your child as a forty-year-old. What does your heart long for as you think of their future?

- What are the values, priorities, and convictions of that future adult?

- What are you doing now to shape who they become?

- How does a biblical worldview get both taught and caught in the home as well as in the church?

Time and Place: Discipleship Is Deliberate

Now that we have defined the vision necessary for church leaders to train and mobilize parents in order to cultivate a culture of discipleship at home, we need to consider the next of our Central Formational Objectives. The vision for discipleship drives direction, making vision the *why*. Then it's only fitting that we look at the *when* or, as we've called it, "time and place." As we begin this section, let's examine the *what* and *why* of time and place in order to understand together how deliberate parents must be.

The What: Inspire and equip families, in light of the gospel, to spend their time and use their space counterculturally.

The Why: The home that prioritizes lifelong faith in Jesus will organically and intentionally arrange their rhythms to consistently engage in discipling their kids.

Time has been called "the Great Equalizer." While we might have various levels of finances, education, experiences, etc., we all have the same number of hours in each day and the same number of days in each week. None of us has a leg up on more time than anyone else. Therefore, as church and ministry leaders, we must be able to walk alongside families in order to view time and place as a resource that should be invested, in light of the gospel, to engage their kids in discipleship. After all, discipleship is deliberate, and, as the apostle Paul wrote in Ephesians, "Look carefully then how you walk, not as unwise but as wise, making the best use of the time, because the days are evil" (Eph. 5:15–16). The word "evil" might sound startling or harsh; after all, there's a lot of good things that families can do these days.

We must remember that anything and everything we put in place of God becomes an idol—that includes the "good things" on which families might spend their time. Soccer can become sacred. Ballet lessons, gymnastic meets, and theater classes can encroach upon the divine design of the home, which isn't unending activity, but deliberate discipleship. Evil doesn't always parade around in obvious attire; sometimes it dresses in opportunities and activities, which, when prioritized, become idols that rob us and the families we serve from putting God at the center of life. We'll get into this more in a bit, but first let's step back and look at the larger picture.

Good and Busy, by the Numbers

Ask the typical parent in your church, or even the typical adult congregant, how they are, and I would imagine they will likely answer one of two responses (or a variation thereof): "good" or "busy." Busy has become a fairly standard response. In fact, for some, busy is a badge of honor; maybe that's true for you. It can feel like we're busier than ever, and while that might feel true, it's worth trying to understand if it is, in fact, true.

According to a 2022 study conducted by the American Survey Center, "a generation ago, family meals were routine. Roughly three-quarters of baby boomers (76 percent) and 84 percent of Americans who belong to the silent generation report that they had meals together as a family every day. Fifty-nine percent of Americans who belong to Generation X say they had daily meals with their family. In contrast, less than half of millennials (46 percent) and Generation Z

(38 percent) report that growing up they had meals with their family every day."[6]

Family meals aren't the be-all and end-all of quality family time, but they can serve as an indicator of health and well-being for the family. While it may seem typical to not eat together on a daily basis, there are more signs about how families spend time together.

For example, in another 2022 survey, this one conducted by the U.S. Bureau of Labor Statistics, "adults living in households with children under age 6 spent an average of 2.1 hours per day providing primary childcare to household children. Adults living in households where the youngest child was between the ages of 6 and 17 spent less than half as much time providing primary childcare to household children—49 minutes per day. Primary childcare is childcare that is done as a main activity, such as providing physical care or reading to children."[7]

Did you see that? *"49 minutes per day."* While we can account for the typical demands of daily time such as school and sleep, it's no wonder why the children of our churches largely aren't being discipled at home; they're getting less than an hour of care daily. When you dig into the data even more, you begin to see that activities such as reading to/with children and talking to/with children average out at .04 hours per day. It's not hard to begin to understand that discipleship in the home is waning when parents and children are reading together and talking together in such small doses.

Busyness is to the home like water is to fish—it is simply the environment we're surrounded by and swimming in. If we don't walk with families in order to inspire and equip them to be more deliberate in how they use their time, they may simply end up drowning under the weight of schedules in a sea of choices. Let's look at some practical ways we can begin to help families swim against the cultural tidal wave of busyness.

The Power of "No"

Our family loves going on vacation. Sometimes we borrow a cabin from dear friends. In the mountains, next to a babbling brook, we'll build fires in the fire pit, play endless rounds of chess, read, and make a ton of food. These vacations are incredibly restorative and wonderful. Even in writing about them, I wish I were in the screened-in porch, feeling the breeze and listening to the creek bubble and babble on by.

Other vacations include going to Disney World. In terms of activities, it's basically the opposite of everything I mentioned above, minus the food . . . there's always way too much food. In truth, we've been to Disney World a lot. When they were young, our kids loved the pool, especially Disney pools! In fact, the selection of the hotel at times was swayed by what the pool was like. However, their desire to swim would often collide with their desire to head into one of the Disney parks and ride rides or shop in the gift stores. There were plenty of times when my wife and I would patiently wait while the four kiddos debated whether they wanted to swim or ride on Big Thunder Railroad. Swim or Magic Kingdom? Magic Kingdom or swim? Back and forth it would go, but then we would remind them that saying "yes" to swimming would be saying "no" to Big Thunder. Neither option was wrong, but we couldn't do both at the same time.

> Busyness is to the home like water is to fish—it is simply the environment we're surrounded by and swimming in.

It was in those times, helping our kids navigate their desires, that my wife and I began to teach them the power of "no." This isn't an original idea to us, as there are many versions of it out there. That said, when our kids fell victim to analysis paralysis based on their desires and seemingly endless options, we had to tell them whatever they said yes to meant they were saying no to everything else. One yes is equivalent to countless no's. It can be easy to say yes to great things, but it's always more difficult to say no to good things.

Saying no to items and options reveals the significance of yes. When we are in a committed relationship, we said no to everyone else, which makes our yes to our significant other even more powerful. When we've committed to a church, we've said no to every other place and people and yes to the family of God that is our local church, imperfections and all! Simply, the power of "no" isn't just in the selection, but in the value it assigns and affirms when we say yes.

Time: Own or Be Owned

Greg McKeown dives into this more in-depth in his masterful work *Essentialism: The Disciplined Pursuit of Less.*[8] McKeown challenges readers to say "yes" to only the most essential and exciting choices that will provide the most benefit. While this sounds easy on the surface, the fact is that for most families, it's hard to determine what gets our emphatic and enthusiastic *Yes!*

Saying yes to family discipleship will require saying no to other commitments. It may mean that families need to reprioritize their activities. It may mean taking a step back from the demands and pressures of those in our neighborhoods and communities to "go and do" in order to consider the desire and invitation of Jesus to "come and follow Me."

To be clear, none of us—Matt, Sam, or I—is saying extracurriculars are bad. There is nothing evil about tee-ball, gymnastics, theater, soccer, or ballet. Park-district activities, school sports, and summer camps are not bad for our kids. What we are saying is that, if we're not intentional, these activities can easily begin to demand more and more of our families, our time, and our allegiances. It simply comes down to a matter of math.

In our home there are four kids. Even when we commit to one activity per child per season, we're committing to hours of practices, miles of driving, days and days of competitions or performances, and before you know it, it can be months since we were able to eat together for consecutive nights in any given week. What does all this mean for families? It's both simple and difficult: families need to realize that they must own the schedule or their schedule will own them.

In his 2011 book *Bursts: The Hidden Pattern Behind Everything We Do*, renowned physicist Albert-László Barabási writes a line that all of us would do well to remember: "Time is our most valuable non-renewable resource, and if we want to treat it with respect, we need to set priorities."[9] Barabási's emphasis on respecting the resource of time assigns the resource the highest value and respect. However, as Bible-believing Christians, we should not confuse the giver of the gift with the gift itself. That said, while time is a nonrenewable resource, it is a resource given to us by God so that like all other resources He provides, we might use it to build His kingdom, and that includes the discipleship of children. So, what does this mean practically?

The Cost of Discipleship

In Luke 14:25–33, Jesus is speaking to the crowds about the cost of being a disciple. While we can romanticize what it might have been like to be part of the original twelve and be in close friendship and fellowship with Jesus while He bodily walked upon the Earth, we must not forget those who physically followed Jesus and left everything to do so. There is a real cost to being a disciple. To illustrate this point, Jesus speaks to the crowds who have gathered around Him about the cost of discipleship. As a masterful teacher, Jesus uses the illustrations of hating one's family (which is to say loving God more), building a tower, and going to war. In all these Jesus is making a point: that discipleship comes at a great cost. This truth hits even harder today!

Considering what it means to follow Jesus means to be fully committed to Him. Parents are uniquely positioned to not only instruct their children in this but also live it out by being committed to saying "yes" and perhaps more importantly "no" to the right things. What are our calendars and commitments describing in terms of our discipleship? Remember what Barabási wrote regarding the resource of time and McKeown wrote regarding priorities? How can we walk with families to fight the temptation of over-involvement in every good activity in which their children may demonstrate interest, or even some skill in, so that they can commit to the greater and lasting priority of discipleship or faith formation in the life of their children? To be sure, there is a very real cost to follow Jesus. It will require us to surrender everything, even our schedules, perhaps even swim lessons or scouting or soccer, but if our schedules are allowed to grow without intention, we will no longer own our calendars, but rather they will own us as well as our families and their faith.

Finding the Right Rhythms

Life is rhythmic. The heart beats, the seasons turn, time marches on. There is rhythm to life, and perhaps no passage of the Bible is more intentional in teaching us this than Ecclesiastes 3:1–8. "For everything there is a season, and a time for every matter under heaven" (v.1). Some of these rhythms are easy to recognize, like mornings and evenings, sunrises and sunsets, the seasons (except perhaps in Santa Monica, where it's almost always 68 and sunny). God designed our lives to have inherent rhythms. As ministry leaders, we can help families recognize and capitalize on these rhythms as they pursue discipleship.

While it might seem silly to consider, one doesn't celebrate a birthday daily, or even weekly. While mothers of newborns measure a baby's age in days, weeks, and months, birthdays are an annual marker of age, and once a child is two, they are rarely referred to as XX months old. The annual rhythm of a birthday is an organic rhythm or a regular repetition built into the larger understanding of time.

Conversely, bedtimes happen daily (praise God). But while this is also an organic rhythm, how a family engages in bedtime can start to be seen as an intentional rhythm or a designed rhythm created by a household in order to provide routine and predictability. Intentional rhythms can happen on a different schedule or regularity than an organic rhythm, and sometimes these rhythms can be harder to spot, but they often can be quicker to employ and yield a more immediate return.

Organic rhythms and intentional rhythms do not have to be mutually exclusive; both can be recognized and used by a family to create a means for habits to take place. Those habits, in turn, form patterns which, over time, create a lifestyle. Rhythms, habits, patterns, and lifestyles—these are the building blocks or practices of discipleship. And when employed regularly (not necessarily expertly), families will begin to be transformed by practicing what author and lawyer Justin Whitmel Earley called "habits of the household"[10] and what John Mark Comer made popular, a "Rule of Life."[11]

Making the Most of Organic Rhythms

When we talk about "organic rhythms," we're talking about the natural milestones, tempos, and timings of events like birthdays (we all have one each year), meals (we all eat), waking up and lying down

(Deuteronomy 6 language). These natural or organic rhythms provide easy opportunities for families to engage in practices. Praying a passage over a child each birthday, dinner conversations with kids on where we saw God throughout the day, morning blessing before heading out to school and work, as well as an evening blessing before bed. These are simple building blocks and routines families can introduce and integrate into their ongoing lives. While starting these can feel awkward, or even messy at times, over time they become the means of discipleship that are simply part of life.

Investing in Intentional Rhythms

Intentional rhythms are the means by which parents make the strategic choice to engage in discipleship with their children. Some intentional rhythms are really, really approachable, such as a parent regularly taking a child to breakfast and simply having a conversation, or rather than listening to music on a car ride, have a question to discuss with a child or look for ways to see God as you drive. Other intentional rhythms can include quiet times together, engaging together in videos (like those from The Bible Project for older kids), working through resources like *The New City Catechism* as a family. Intentional rhythms are often enhanced by experiences or resources, so at times these may require an investment, but there is no greater ROI than what John describes in 3 John 4, "I have no greater joy than to hear that my children are walking in the truth."

We spoke in chapter 5 about rites of passage. Helping families create rites of passage is an incredible and meaningful way to invest in intentional rhythms. It also can be incorporated into your ministry as a means to build belonging. Whether it's celebrating salvation, baptisms, Step-Up Sunday, commemorating the first lost tooth, or (for those in more of a traditional church background) first communion and confirmation, rites of passage create ceremonies of celebration as well as establish landmarks to look back upon.

There is no one I know who can currently speak to this subject, especially for fathers and sons, more than Jon Tyson. Jon pastors Church of the City New York and his work on raising boys to become men is phenomenal.[12] I've used it with my own son. The rites of passage he helps fathers discover and design are intentional rhythms that create a road map, not only toward manhood, but discipleship. Designing rites of passage in your ministry and emphasizing them with families will help parents create meaningful moments on the journey of discipleship.

Putting Discipleship in Its Place

A brief word on place before we move on. Forming disciples happens in the midst of life, not outside of it. There is no sacred space or place where discipleship happens. "Sitting in your house," "walking by the way," "lying down," "rising up," "doorposts," "gates," "all the world"—these and more are the places the Bible mentions where discipleship happens. Jesus formed disciples from twelve young men while walking, eating, serving, teaching, on boats, on hillsides, in the bad part of town, everywhere and anywhere.

> Forming disciples happens in the midst of life, not outside of it.

Everywhere and anywhere is the right place for parents to disciple their children. Kitchen islands, dining room tables, road trips, playgrounds, backyards, food courts, school pick-up lines, naptimes, mornings, evenings, anytime, and anyplace. Your role in this is to help parents identify these opportunities, but this is like helping little ones at an egg hunt! You're simply going to show them where to find these sweet moments, right there, in the open.

Anytime and anyplace is perfect for parents to disciple their children. As we move into the next section, use the following questions to help the parents and families you serve consider when and where they can disciple their kids.

Helpful Questions for Parents to Consider

- How does your family make decisions regarding what to say "yes" to?

- If you were to audit a typical week, how much time is taken up by activities?

- If you could press reset on your calendar, given the goal of forming children with lasting faith in Jesus, what would you do differently?

- What's one activity or commitment that you would say no to right now if you could?

- What are some natural rhythms in your home where faith formation can easily take place?

Language: Discipleship as Dialogue

Up to this point, we've looked at the *why* behind child discipleship in the home (vision). We've also taken time to unpack *when* and *where* parents can form a child's faith (time and place). However, it's often common for parents—even the ones who deeply desire to disciple their children, even the ones who you might think know everything there is to know about the Christian faith—to feel inadequate regarding exactly how to form the faith of their children. So, let's take a closer look at the *how* of home discipleship and consider language.

The What: Model for parents how to integrate dynamic conversations in the home in a way that speaks to the presence of Jesus in their everyday lives.

The Why: The home that leverages the power of conversation to foster faith in Jesus understands that dialogue is foundational for child discipleship.

Parents have a lot on their plate. As we covered in the previous section, the typical family is incredibly busy and parents often play the role of chauffeur, activity director, short-order cook, at-home physician, disciplinarian, wardrobe specialist, housekeeper, laundry hero, and so much more. It's no wonder why conversations between parents and kids often seem more like questions and answers or permissions and denials and less like dynamic conversations. Simply, no one teaches parents how to have a true dialogue with their kids! If you're a parent, think about how you might address your child and contrast that with how you might talk with a neighbor or coworker. There's probably a big difference. And when we consider the fact that not only have parents not been taught how to talk with their children, let alone disciple their children through dialogue, it's little wonder that the home is facing a discipleship deficit.

More than a Monologue

When we think about discipleship, it can be tempting to think about it *only* as teaching or proclamation, especially when it comes to discipling children. As Christians, we are people of the Word. God spoke and all creation was made. Jesus is the "Word made flesh." We join the psalmist in desiring that the "words of [our] mouth and meditation of [our] heart be acceptable" to God (Ps. 19:14). It can be easy to conclude that discipleship is monologue rather than dialogue.

However, this doesn't seem to be the way Jesus discipled the Twelve.

Throughout the Gospels, Jesus doesn't just speak *to* people, but rather Jesus speaks *with* people. The Bible records that Jesus asks over 300 questions and is asked more than 130 questions. If anyone could have simply preached and proclaimed, it would have been Jesus. The Word became flesh and dwelt among us. He alone would have all authority, every answer, and the right to simply talk and teach all about the kingdom of heaven, repentance of sin, the nuances of the Hebrew Scriptures, and to be sure, He does . . . yet Jesus seemed to understand that dialogue and discussion was much more effective in forming lasting faith. He models for pastors, parents, and leaders the fact that, in a relational context, dialogue is vital in forming faith.

In John 4, we read about a revival. Any Christian would love to be part of such a tremendous work of God that results in the multitude from a region coming to faith. But how did this work start? Was it the product of Jesus preaching to the crowds? Did the disciples begin simply telling people about the Messiah? No, revival comes to the region of the Middle East then known as Samaria because a woman at a well, riddled with shame and wanting to redirect Jesus from exposing her pain, wasn't shamed by Jesus and preached at. Rather Jesus and this woman had a conversation, which broke a number of social and societal norms in Jesus' context. It was through a dialogue—questions and answers—that this woman came to saving faith in Christ that would then lead to "Many Samaritans from that town believed in him because of the woman's testimony," and "many more believed because of his word" (John 4:39, 41).

As John writes earlier in his gospel in John 1:14, "the Word became flesh," but didn't dictate to us; rather Jesus "dwelt among us." Jesus didn't arrive to only dictate and declare, but to discuss and dialogue with people in the midst of their questions, confusion, and need.

We Make It Harder than It Needs to Be

More than "Do what I say," discipleship is the conversational means of faith formation every family must engage in. When the now-well-known command was given to the nation of Israel in Deuteronomy 6, the precedent to "teach them diligently" wasn't given only to the Bible-college trained or seminary graduates. This command from God was given to *every* family in Israel to be done everywhere. God didn't command and doesn't tell His people to do something they cannot do, whether by their own means or through faith.

The parents you serve view you as "the professional" when it comes to discipleship conversations, so it's going to be up to you, children's ministry leader, to equip them to talk *with* their kids about Jesus, about what they read in the Bible, about prayer and practices. And here's the thing: the bar isn't too high. Parents don't have to teach their preschooler words or phrases like "hypostatic union," "substitutionary atonement," or "theophany," but they do need to have even the simplest of conversations about God's love, Jesus as their Good Shepherd, and the fact that the church is a family. Equally, it's important for parents of older kids to not just expect blind obedience for faith in Christ without dialogue. Like the old saying goes, if someone can talk you into it, someone else can talk you out of it. It is worth repeating: discipleship is the conversational means of faith formation every family must engage in.

Look, Listen, and Share

Have you ever needed a car and then, after doing the research, test-driving, and speaking with those you trust, decide on the exact make and model you wanted? If so, undoubtedly, once you made that decision, I would be willing to wager that you started seeing that car everywhere. I know we had that experience! The truth isn't necessarily that there were more Ford Expeditions on the road once we decided to buy ours, but rather we were more aware of their presence, and therefore they seemed more present in our lives. The same is true with God. When we look for His love, His power, and His truth, we tend to find it. However, we need to be quick to share these everyday evidences of God with those around us, especially the children in our lives! Some call this testifying, others call this God-spotting; whatever you want to call it, it's the act of declaring the reality of God and His attributes in our world that matters.

This simple, yet profound act is not only nice to do with kids, but necessary as it relates to forming lasting faith. Imagine the dinner conversations that can be had daily when families are joyfully telling one another about where they saw God move in their classrooms and on their commutes. Consider the day-after-day body of evidence that would be formed with each dinner table discussion, and each car-line pickup conversation when families dialogue about where the love of Jesus was shown in lunchrooms, locker rooms and throughout the everyday life of a family.

Discussion Makes Sense of Discovery

It is certainly easier to talk to rather than with somebody, especially kids. If you've spent time talking with kids, you've experienced the uncanny way in which a child can offer non sequitur after non sequitur. The conversation you began with a child by asking them the question: "What was one highlight of your day at school?" can meander its way to their favorite insect and keep going until somehow the conversation landed on you both talking about the differences in mittens and gloves or why our galaxy is called the Milky Way. I know in our home, our four kids can take a conversation in seemingly endless directions. It would be interesting to hire a stenographer to keep notes of our dinner conversations, read back what we talked about when we sat down, and consider where the conversation stopped at the end of dinner.

All kidding aside, parents must realize the gift and importance of conversations as an essential tool of forming lasting faith in Jesus in the hearts and minds of children. From the youngest of ages, moms and dads, grandparents, and others can begin talking to children about all the wonderful, beautiful things God made and in doing so start to inform children about who God is, what He can do, how He loves them, and more.

Matt tells a story about how his wife, Katie, was outside with their oldest son, Warren, when he was still a newborn. With Warren in her arms, Katie was pointing to the trees in their yard and letting Warren feel the veins and stem of a leaf. Katie, using some very practical and beautiful wisdom, explained to Warren that God made this leaf, and it came from a tree that God also made. She went on to gently and sweetly tell Warren that God was powerful, kind, and wise. Even though Warren was still an infant and in no way capable of understanding ecology, biology, or even what a leaf was, Katie knew that it's never too early to begin talking about God, even to the youngest of hearts. Those small moments and simple discoveries helped lay a foundation for faith formation conversations.

Weaving Together an Understanding of Faith in Jesus

In 2009, Awana executive Larry Fowler released a book on child discipleship called *Raising a Modern Joseph*.[13] Fowler drew from the life of Joseph five attributes of a disciple and went on through the book to identify which age and stage each attribute could begin to be formed in a child's life. As a means to give practical advice to help train parents to talk and listen to their children in order to form lasting faith, I'm going to build upon Fowler's work.

The attributes Fowler identified were eventually named "Life Threads" with the idea that, when woven together, they would ultimately produce a tapestry of discipleship in the life of children and youth. Categorized in five areas, these Life Threads help give structure to what children can learn about the doctrines of Christian faith at what ages. Please know, as we think about our ministries as well as the families we serve and each child in our churches and communities, it would be ludicrous to think about these as prescriptive. Each child in each family is different. Allow these Life Threads to serve as description rather than prescription.

1. **Wonder:** The youngest of children can begin to develop a wonder of God. Paul notes in Romans 1 that God's power and attributes are present in creation. This is exactly what was happening in the account I shared about Katie and Warren. Having discussions with children where questions are being asked and answered about the trees, the sky, the sun, about the creation all around them will help young hearts begin to grasp the wonder of who God is and what He's capable of. This will lead to awe of not only God's power, but also His love for us.

2. **Wisdom:** Young children are especially good at asking "why," and what a great way to have conversations not just about who God is, but why He does what He does! Young minds and hearts can begin to grasp that God is wise, and in doing so, they too can begin to gain wisdom. Each question as to "why" provides an open door to wonderful discussions parents and leaders can begin to steer children to understand God and His wonderful wisdom.

3. **Grace:** As children begin to grow, they begin to realize all is not right with the world. Even in the first five minutes of most Disney princess movies, we see that something bad has happened, whether a parent died or an evil power has taken over, or some other injustice has occurred and needs to be made right. Unfortunately, it doesn't take long for children to begin to see that there is something broken in this world. We mustn't try and simply sugarcoat this. With love and wisdom, we must define this brokenness for what it is: the effects of sin. Enter the grace found in Jesus! Building upon the wonder a child can grasp about who God is and the wisdom of how God works in this world, is the grace He shows through Jesus. Conversations about forgiveness, consequence, love, mercy, and grace are part of the beauty of dialogue with an elementary-aged child.

4. **Purpose:** Remember thinking about what you wanted to be when you grew up? As children consider the fact that they're growing, they begin to innocently and beautifully ask questions and find it fun to think about what they want to do when they're big. While it's easy to think about this in terms of a profession (who didn't want to be a zookeeper or a marine biologist?), it's much more formational to direct these conversations around not just what a child will do when they're older, but who will they become. Careers come and go, but character and purpose are definitive, and God has a lot to say about who we are that should inform what we do.

5. **Perspective:** If purpose has to do with us and who we are, perspective is about where we fit in terms of God's sovereignty. In Awana leadership discussions we often talk about God's

sovereignty and our responsibility. Yes, God is sovereign and yes, we are responsible. Talking with, not just dictating to, kids and teens about God's sovereignty, especially as they're walking through their adolescent and teen years is crucial in setting them up with faith that can endure. Our doubts about God often come down to misunderstandings of His sovereignty and our responsibility.

In an age where we often default to digital communication (perhaps, like me, you've texted your spouse from one part of the house to another), we must be deliberate about the fact that dialogue is foundational for discipleship. It's not just about monologuing children to faith in Jesus, it's about the journey of conversation.

Consider the fact that Jesus, like the rabbis of His time, spent countless hours with His young disciples. While we read of times of instruction, we also read of discussions He had. I am sure we can safely conjecture that there were countless conversations between Jesus and His young followers around dinner tables, and while they walked from one town to another. In every seemingly mundane moment, it's not hard to imagine Jesus speaking *with*, not just to, His followers. Perhaps it's in Jesus' relationship with twelve young men and others whom He had relationships with that we see a living out of Deuteronomy 6, specifically the Great Shema. It was through discussions along the road, around the fire, in the mornings and in the evenings that Peter, James, John, and the others were speaking with Jesus, learning from Him,processing with Him, growing in their love for God. But not just through declaration, but dialogue steeped in conversation and questions, formed in the back and forth among one another.

You can help parents have meaningful conversations with their children, turning everyday moments into dialogues of discipleship that shape hearts and minds. Make it easy, make it likely, make it known that even the smallest and simplest of exchanges can make a lifetime of difference. And make it a goal that the families you serve do more than know that while faith comes by hearing, discipleship comes through dialogue.

Helpful Questions for Parents to Consider

- Are you looking for ways every day to have conversations with your children that ultimately speak to who God is?

- What are some rites of passage children's ministries and families can design to create intentional rhythms?

- Are we trained to spot God and training our kids to do the same?

- Are you more prone to simply talk to your kids about the truths of the Bible rather than engage with them in discussion? Why or why not?

- Are you asking your children open-ended questions about where they're seeing God? Are you sharing with them areas where you're seeing God as well?

Community: Discipleship Takes a Team

We've covered a lot of ground as we've discovered the four Central Formational Objectives and the role each plays in answering the question, "How can church leaders train and mobilize parents to cultivate a culture of discipleship at home?" Thus far we've looked at vision (the why), time and place (the when and where), and language (the how) of faith formation in the home. When employed, these key factors will help parents make significant strides in discipling their children. However, there is one more objective we have yet to cover and it is the aspect of *who*. Who is it that we need to help disciple our children? The answer is simple: a community; after all, discipleship takes a team.

Like we've done previously, let's look at the what and the why of this objective together. The following will help us understand the *what* of community as it relates to faith formation in the home as well as why it matters:

What: Impress upon parents the value in a team of intentional relationships for the discipleship of every child.

Why: The home that builds a discipleship team around each child creates multiple connection points that form a foundation of Christian faith.

Let's unpack this together.

In the mid 1990s, then-First Lady Hillary Rodham Clinton made famous an old African proverb, "It takes a village to raise a child."[14] As a teen in the mid-'90s (it isn't lost on me that this was in the previous century), I can remember hearing this everywhere I went, from school to church and eventually at college. It seemed that Mrs. Clinton had tapped into a core truth that was being forgotten: that healthy children were the result of a network of care, beyond just the home.

It might help to contextualize what life was like when Mrs. Clinton offered this to the American public. America was becoming older as those from the Greatest Generation were beginning to retire and baby boomers were hitting their stride. The Hispanic population was also growing five times as fast as the rest of the population, and began to emerge as a stronger political force. Grunge and alternative choices of lifestyle were more mainstream and accessible than before thanks to cable news and wider media distribution. Last, but not least, this was at a time in the 1990s when the divorce rate in the US was at an all-time high.

According to data from the National Center for Family & Marriage Research, divorces among adults in the US grew to their highest rates in the 1980s and 1990s.[15] The brokenness in the traditional American family, linked to the passing of "No Fault" divorce laws at the state level, led to an increase in single-parent homes and saw rising trends in gang activity, substance abuse, and addiction as well as an introduction of cultural phrases like "latchkey kid," "the war on drugs," "drug abuse resistance education or DARE," and others that were endemic of that era. Society sensed something was broken in the US at this time and Mrs. Clinton did her best to define it as well as provide a solution when she offered the African axiom.

> If it takes a village to raise a child, we would offer that it takes a team to disciple one.

If it takes a village to raise a child, we would offer that it takes a team to disciple one.

Home Team

In 2016, history was made. The Chicago Cubs won the MLB World Series for the first time since 1908. For more than a century, people lived and died in the Chicago area waiting for a roster to be assembled that could compete to bring home a championship to the North Side. As a Chicago-area native and a Cubs fan by birth, I was all too familiar with the hope and eventual pain every season would bring. "There's always next year," was the perennial mantra of hopeful disappointment.

However, the Cubs winning the World Series didn't just happen in 2016; the road to get there began in earnest in 2011 when the Ricketts family (majority owner of the Chicago Cubs) acquired Theo

Epstein from the Boston Red Sox to fulfill the role of president of baseball operations.[16] Epstein began to construct a roster through acquisitions, drafts, and trades that would eventually lead to breaking one of the longest championship droughts in sports history—something so meaningful to generations of Cubs fans that it's taking me every bit of determination to not write more about this because I care so deeply about those readers for whom sports analogies fail to capture their heart or convey truth. Suffice to say teams matter—just ask the millions of Cubs fans who lived and died watching their "loveable losers" never win the pennant.

The point of telling you about the greatest team in baseball history (as a Yankees fan, Sam would strongly disagree with this) is to state that it takes the building of a team to accomplish a lasting impact. It's true in sports, and it's especially true in discipling children to follow Jesus for a lifetime. It's not so much that you build a team; after all there are plenty of teams in plenty of leagues that lose each season. Effective teams are more than just players who share the field or court at the same time; rather they are a strategically constructed group of talented individuals, united for a shared cause or purpose with complementary strengths in order to achieve at a high level.

Parents need to be even more strategic than the management of a professional sports franchise in constructing a team around their children. No one becomes a disciple in isolation; just like no single player wins the championship in a team sport, a team needs to be constructed to fill in the gaps, combine their unique talents, and ultimately win, together. Championships are good, but disciples are timeless.

A Sudden Left Turn: Alone, Together

From eternity past, God has existed in perfect, trinitarian community. In three persons, God the Father, God the Son, and God the Holy Spirit crafted all creation, are rescuing people from sin and death, and will renew and reconcile all things. Community and divine fellowship are indivisible from Christianity; it's within the divine DNA, yet in the twenty-first-century evangelical West, and in most of the Western world, isolation and loneliness are the norm.

While national rates of loneliness have dropped since mid-2020, the US Surgeon General has launched a multifaceted program to combat the effects of what is termed "the loneliness epidemic." According to reports, the effects of loneliness are comparable to smoking fifteen cigarettes a day.[17] In addition, it is the leading cause of suicide. Add to this the fact that many young people ages eighteen through twenty-four are experiencing the highest comparable rates of loneliness, and we can begin to see that this isn't an "out there threat" like those we used to talk about in the 1990s when technology wasn't nearly as embedded in our lives as it is today. Loneliness is pervasive.

Before we think that this is someone else's problem in our church, loneliness is affecting the children we're trying to reach and disciple as well. According to the National Center for School Mental Health, in 2021, "25 percent of girls reported having made a suicide plan."[18] Think about your children's or youth ministry and consider for a moment that statistically a quarter of the girls you see on a weekend service or during midweek have a plan to end their life. Let's pause here for a moment and let that sink in.

There are seemingly countless factors that contribute to the loneliness our children are being formed in. From the increase in social media and technology use to the rise of hyper-individualism to the long-term effects of the COVID-19 pandemic on our social activities, the loneliness epidemic is multifaceted and increasingly painful. Yet the factors have been in place for well over a decade.

In her 2010 work, re-released in 2017, *Alone Together*, Sherry Turkle states how we've grown lonelier as a society despite the increased connectivity that technology has provided by social media platforms as well as elements such as text messaging and email. Turkle states, "Digital connections . . . offer the illusion of companionship without the demands of friendship."[19] While the digital technologies we rely on for our daily lives make connectivity more available, our lives are not better for it. Perhaps it would be good to realize that while digital technology was created for us, we are not created for it.

If we believe that we are made in the image of God and that we share in His attributes, it should be no surprise to understand that humans need others. We are relational by design. Friendships are formational, especially for children. It's social activities, personal relationships, and face-to-face interactions that act as water over the rock and form the contours of our lives and identities. Even more formational than peer-to-peer relationships are those that include mentorship.

> "Digital connections offer the illusion of companionship without the demands of friendship."

Every Child Needs a Team

No matter your role, if you work with children and youth, you know the power of meaningful connection in the life of a child. Perhaps God used that loving, caring adult in your life to form a vision and calling for you to work with the next generation, even in a volunteer role. I want to say two things to you.

First, thank you. Thank you for prayerfully taking the time to love kids with the love of Jesus. Thank you for seeing kids, for allowing them to belong, especially for those who find it difficult to belong anywhere. Thank you for the minutes and hours you spend each day committed to leading kids to Jesus and walking with them as they walk with Christ. You are accomplishing so much more than you know.

Second, let me acknowledge that *You can't do this alone!* No one can, especially parents! Why did you just read pages and pages about loneliness? Because the families we serve are swimming in the waters of isolation and disconnection. Even the busiest of families, committed to the team sports and clubs, are likely feeling alone at the deepest levels. Allow me to speak on behalf of the parents in your church . . . *We need help!* But the help we need is more than a handout; we need your help to form a team.

Before you think this is another thing you, church staff member, are ultimately responsible for, let me say this isn't totally on you. However, ministry leaders make for tremendous team members in the lives of every child. Your role in this is two-fold. First, equipping parents to understand that felt need that they can't do it alone isn't something to be ashamed of, it's right! It's actually divine! You get to be the advocate that every parent needs, the one who speaks the truth in love that they need a team to walk with them in discipling their child.

The second role you serve is helping them get some of the teammates in place. These should be the leaders and volunteers you have in your ministry. Rarely does someone who comes to faith as a child remember the sermon or the prayer they prayed . . . they almost *always* remember the loving, caring adult who walked with them to Jesus. Our volunteers need to be more than just warm bodies; they need to be committed to Jesus and forming disciples. Discipleship isn't only showing up consistently, though. Discipleship is a shared journey of faith formation over a span of time. Your ability to recruit the right people is foundational not only in the discipleship of children, but you're also loading the roster of home teams for the families of your church.

Team, Not Task Force

So, what does this look like? It's actually quite simple. Parents need to take stock of the adults in their children's lives or those in close proximity to their families and play a little fantasy football in order to create a team of people around their children. In some denominations, the basis of this is the role of godparents. I had a set and they were always involved in our lives. Godparents can be great, and if you're part of a denomination or tradition that involves them, it's a great place to start bringing this concept of home team into fruition.

If you need to, start from scratch with parents in your church. Allow this to be thought of as who are the most likely people they would like to see their children emulate and learn from. Moment of honesty here, Matt is one of the men who speaks into my son's life. Why did I ask for this from Matt? Because his walk with Jesus is that which I would love for my son Griffin to emulate. There are other men too that I've asked to be part of Griffin's formation process. I asked each because they are men whom Griffin can learn from and whose character can serve as a godly influence in Griffin's life.

The creation of the home team around each child is the culmination of relationships that parents grant access to their children and may specifically ask them to speak into them from time to time. These could be family members, neighbors, coaches, teachers, ministry leaders, mentors, etc. The key is that one is forming a team of individuals they would want to see their child become like. The emphasis here is that this is a team, not a task force, meaning that these individuals are not tasked with achieving a shared goal due to their unique expertise. This also isn't a committee that instructs parents on how to raise their children, though at times they may express a concern if it comes up in a child's life and poses a threat. This is a team, formed to form lasting faith in Jesus in the life of the child.

There may be times when a parent calls on this team for prayer, or guidance, or to ask a couple of them to encourage their child in times of anxiety or stress. This team of people may or may not have any knowledge of one another, but as long as they know and love Jesus as well as know and love the child, this is the base of making an informed choice on assembling the right team.

Sometimes a child can make these connections themselves. Carrie, Pat and Amy, Swang, Harry, Michael, Jared, and Daryl were some of the members of my home team. Though they weren't intentionally selected by my parents to be part of my life, each played a critical role in my discipleship and each helped me grow into the Christ follower I am today.

Even the best home, led by the most biblically minded and intentional parents, cannot fully disciple their kids without the participation of others. Every child in every family needs a team, and while that team roster might change from time to time or at different ages, the key to successful faith formation will be found in the consistency of having multiple, trusted, godly voices speaking into the lives of each child in each home.

Helpful Questions for Parents to Consider

- Who are you doing life with? Are there people you can call in the middle of the night if you need something?

- Who are the leaders you would love to see your child emulate? Perhaps they're local, perhaps they're somewhere else, but as you think about your child, who would you like to see them become like?

- How are you going to set expectations for the home team to come around your child? What are the natural rhythms that exist and how can you capitalize on them?

Simple Math and Profound Impact

The family who is committed to the church and tries to come every Sunday is a growing anomaly. Even in the most committed of congregations, life has a way to pull families out the door. Sometimes it's sickness, sometimes vacations, sometimes it's sports. Whatever the reason, the reality is there are far fewer families earning perfect attendance awards for weekend worship. So rather than bemoan or balk at that reality, let's accept it as less-than-ideal fact.

However, if you feel your family or the families in your church don't follow these norms, let's consider the following. Let's say the children in your church never miss a Sunday, and let's suppose that your church's Sunday school or children's ministry is about an hour or so. That means that the child is spending one hour out of the 168 hours of a given week in church. With this math, we need to understand the home has so much more potential for the discipleship of children given the amount of time a child isn't in our churches, even those with perfect attendance!

Together we've spent considerable time with the question, "How can church leaders train and mobilize parents to cultivate a culture of discipleship at home?" In order to answer this, we've unpacked the four Central Formational Objectives: vision (why), time and place (when and where), language (how) and community (who). Our hope is that you're able to use the questions at the end of each section to begin to walk alongside parents and those raising children in your ministry and church community in order to do the deep, meaningful, eternal work of faith formation. God has placed you in the ministry in which you're currently serving in order to resource and equip the families in your congregation to disciple their children. You are the best partner a parent can have!

Friends, no matter how it may feel, as ministry leaders, specifically in the realm of children's, youth, or next generation, the parents of the children and youth we serve are not the enemy; they are our partners with more access, more responsibility to the children in our ministries. We must walk toward them and then walk alongside them. The home is the best formational partner any church can have when thinking about discipling a child with lasting, resilient faith in Jesus Christ. Allow me to close this chapter with a blessing from Paul to the believers in Galatia.

> And let us not grow weary of doing good, for in due season we will reap, if we do not give up. So then, as we have opportunity, let us do good to everyone, and especially to those who are of the household of faith. (Gal. 6:9–10)

Commissioning

SAM: Fire is a powerful thing. I have seen the damage it can do firsthand. I serve as our city's fire chaplain, so I know the destruction can be devastating. I have comforted families who have lost all they own except the clothes on their backs. Conversely, I also live not far from one of the oldest glass factories in America. From that factory, artisans use fire to refine and shape raw materials to create something beautiful.

We tend to hear mostly of house fires or wildfires and, thus, associate fire with destruction. Scripture doesn't do that. Scripture doesn't fit the neat categories we so often try to fit it into. Fire has a dual purpose in the Bible: to destroy and to refine. There are things that will be destroyed and were destroyed, but there are others that were refined by fire.

In this book, you have heard our passionate plea to move from old maps of entertainment and Bible Lite strategies to a new map dominated by intentional, interpersonal discipleship of the next generation. We learned of the need to be present with kids rather than clever in our techniques. This is not easy to do because it goes against the flow of culture and because it requires us to remove the unnecessary and refine the good, the true, and the beautiful.

You were also given statistics and real-world examples of how vital the work is that you are called to do where God has called you to do it. The need for child discipleship has never been more necessary.

Finally, you were given a new map that is radically focused on the Great Commission and the next generation with practical wisdom and guidelines to engage parents to lead and disciple well.

Our final challenge to you is to *remove* and *refine*. There are things you are doing that you need to stop doing. There are other things you need to refine, and still others that need a new beginning. Do not take our words and use them to burn your programs to the ground. We are passionately telling you to be led by Scripture, to be sensitive to God's Spirit, and to use the wisdom you have acquired and the wisdom of teams.

You may be tempted as a result of this book to quit, to change everything, or to move on as is. Don't do any of those things. Rather, here is what timeless insight tells us to do:

1. **Pray for wisdom to lead well:** Ask God to give you wisdom to guide your conversations as you train parents, volunteers, your team, and those who lead you well. If you are reading this book, you are a leader, and you are ultimately accountable to God for those you shepherd.

2. **Do something:** *I thought you just said don't change everything*, you might be thinking. Yes, *don't* burn it all down. But we would challenge you to take one thing from each chapter of this book and write it on the bottom of the last page as an action item. Or, on the page after this conclusion write one thing

you can change tomorrow, then in six months from now, then a year from now, and finally something you don't think you can ever change that you pray will. We serve a God who does the impossible (Luke 1:37).

3. **Share what you have learned:** Don't keep these truths to yourself. Share them with team members, your lead pastor, parents, and other child discipleship pastors like yourself. We need help knowing what to remove and what to refine. We also need accountability to make those desired changes a reality.

4. **Be courageous:** The process of removal and refinement takes courage. Fire can hurt and heal, but it's never comfortable. Here is a beautiful and comforting truth: Courage for us as Christians is not something that comes from us; it comes to us from outside of us. Courage is a gift. Our natural state, much like sheep, is fear. God, our Good Shepherd, comes to us. His voice from outside us says, "Fear not."

Matthew 28:18–22 is one of the greatest Scriptures in the Bible about discipleship, and it is well-known.

> And Jesus came and said to them, "All authority in heaven and on earth has been given to me. Go therefore and make disciples of all nations, baptizing them in the name of the Father and of the Son and of the Holy Spirit, teaching them to observe all that I have commanded you. And behold, I am with you always, to the end of the age."

You probably skipped that passage because you know it by heart. Go back and reread it because even though you know it well, how it ends is often forgotten. We know that all authority is God's, and we know that we are called to make disciples of all nations. We tend to forget the power by which this takes place. We're all called to *go*. We are told to *make disciples*. We must be reminded that we don't do this alone.

> We're all called to *go*. We are told to *make disciples*. We must be reminded that we don't do this alone.

If you are reading this and you feel like the only person who sees the need for child discipleship—you are not alone. If you are from a small church and you are short on time and resources—you are not alone. If you are discouraged—you are not alone. God has promised He will be with you until the end of the age. What a promise. What a Savior.

Final Note: If you have enjoyed this book and would like to move this conversation from these pages into real-life-in-the-room relational conversations, Matt, Sam, and Mike invite you to join us each year at the Child Discipleship Forum. The forum is a gathering place to discuss child discipleship in today's world. Learn more at www.ChildDiscipleshipForum.com. See you there!

Acknowledgments

WE WOULD LIKE TO THANK all of those who have gone before us: Those who helped draft the old maps that led us to where we are today, those who remained faithful, and those who co-labor in the most important work on the planet—biblical child discipleship.

We clearly didn't get here on our own. We are indebted to a great number of faithful people, and we are standing on the shoulders of outstanding churches, ministries, organizations, and institutions. We'd like to thank those who inspired our thinking:

First and foremost, Jesus Christ our King who has opened our eyes to significant insights. We also thank our wives and ministry partners: Katie Markins, Erin Handler, and Sandra Luce for your wisdom, conversation, humor, friendship, and faithfulness.

Next, to those who have significantly impacted our thinking like Jimmy Mellado of Compassion International; Barna Group; numerous friends in Christian higher education; the Child Discipleship Forum community; our *RESILIENT* readership; the leadership and community of Redeemer Church in Utica, NY; the children's ministry leaders and pastors who dare to ask the hard questions; and various works by John Mark Comer, Mark Sayers, David Kinnaman, Mark Matlock, Gabe Lyons, Tony Evans, Kara Powell, Albert Mohler, Christian Smith, Francis Schaeffer, Darren Whitehead, Jon Tyson,

Dallas Willard, Fred Rogers, George Barna, Dietrich Bonhoeffer, Pete Scazzero, Andy Crouch, Sean McDowell, Tim Keller, and Ed Stetzer.

We also thank the Awana team and community who live out the vision and mission: Kevin White, Brian Rhodes, Kevin Orris, Stephen Maphosah, Ed Gossien, Steve Cohoon, Beth Bedoe, Chip Root, Ken Toeller, Kellie Bartley, Tim Sandvall, Colin Robinson, Yeli Acevedo, Tom Chilton, Melanie Hester, Alicia Tracy, Gajendra Tamang, Sarah Dudt, Miguel Perez, Elinor Kinnier, Mark Campbell, Peter Mayberry, Dan Lovaglia, Mark McPeak, Casey Pointious, Norm Whitney, the Awana Board of Directors, and so many others.

Much of our research is funded by the generosity of our donors. You are true ministry partners. We are beyond grateful for you and we love you deeply. What could be more important than investing in forming the faith of our children?

Notes

Chapter 1: We're Using Old Maps

1. Julia Buckley, "Cruise Ship Runs Aground During Caribbean Voyage," CNN, March 17, 2022, https://www.cnn.com/travel/article/norwegian-escape-cruise-runs-aground/index.html.

2. John Mark Comer and Mark Sayers, hosts, "An Interview with Jon Tyson," May 28, 2019, *This Cultural Moment* podcast, season, episode 14.

3. Paulo Forlani, "Universale Descrittione Di Tutta la Terra Conosciuta Fin Qui," 1565, http://www.myoldmaps.com/renaissance-maps-1490-1800/398-forlani.pdf.

4. Ross Cochran and Matt Markins, hosts, with David Kinnaman, "Generation Z: How the Church Is 'Woefully Unprepared' and What You Can Do About it," September 9, 2021, *Child Discipleship* podcast, episode 92.

5. David Kinnaman and Mark Matlock, *Faith for Exiles: 5 Ways for a New Generation to Follow Jesus in Digital Babylon* (Grand Rapids, MI: Baker Books, 2019), 32.

Chapter 2: A Little Less Disney, A Bit More Mister Rogers

1. Fred Rogers, "The Messages," Mister Rogers' Neighborhood, https://www.misterrogers.org/the-messages/.

2. Neil Postman, *Amusing Ourselves to Death: Public Discourse in the Age of Show Business* (New York: Penguin, 2005), Kindle.

3. Sherry Turkle, *Reclaiming Conversation: The Power of Talk in a Digital Age* (New York: Penguin, 2015), Kindle, 12.

4. Sherry Turkle, *Alone Together: Why We Expect More from Technology and Less from Each Other* (New York: Basic Books, 2017).

5. "Remembering Mr. Rogers (1994/1997)," Charlie Rose, February 27, 2016, video, 02:30, https://www.youtube.com/watch?v=djoyd46TVVc.

6. MarquetteU, "Fred Rogers' Commencement Address at Marquette University," May 15, 2018, video, 13:50, https://youtu.be/qdcEGvk5764.

7. Ibid.

8. Tom Junod, "Can You Say . . . Hero," *Esquire Magazine*, April 6, 2017, www.esquire.com/entertainment/tv/a27134/can-you-say-hero-esq1198/.

9. Sam Luce, "Is Excellence Killing the Church?," blog, May 25, 2017, Sam-Luce.com, https://samluce.com/2017/05/is-excellence-killing-the-church/.

10. Fred Rogers, *You Are Special* (New York: Penguin, 1995), Kindle, 99.

11. Eugene H. Peterson, *A Long Obedience in the Same Direction: Discipleship in an Instant Society* (Downer's Grove, IL: IVP Books, 1980), Kindle.

12. Rogers, *You Are Special*, 26.

13. Dietrich Bonhoeffer, *Life Together and Prayerbook of the Bible* (Minneapolis, MN: Fortress, 2004), Kindle, 98.

14. Rogers, *You Are Special*, 105.

15. Ibid., 136.

Chapter 3: The Old Map of Children's Ministry

1. AnnaMarie Houlis, "How to Drive Urgency at Work (Without Relying on Fear)," Fairygodboss, September 24, 2019, https://www.fairygodboss.com/career-topics/burning-platform.

2. Scott D. Anthony, "How to Anticipate a Burning Platform," *Harvard Business Review*, December 11, 2012, hbr.org/2012/12/how-to-anticipate-a-burning-platform.

3. Carey Nieuwhof and David Kinnaman, hosts, "Children's Ministry and How to Make Resilient Child Disciples with Awana CEO Matt Markins," April 27, 2022, *Church Pulse Weekly Podcast,* episode 111.

4. Ibid.

5. Gary McIntosh and Paul Engle eds., *Evaluating the Church Growth Movement: 5 Views* (Grand Rapids, MI: Zondervan, 2004).

6. Formerly known as Q Ideas, https://events.thinqmedia.com/culturesummit.

7. Greg Hawkins and Cally Parkinson, *MOVE: What 1,000 Churches Reveal About Spiritual Growth* (Grand Rapids, MI: Zondervan, 2011).

8. Ibid.

9. Matt Markins, Dan Lovaglia, and Mark McPeak, *The Gospel Truth About Children's Ministry* (Streamwood, IL: Awana, 2014), 53.

10. Valerie Bell, Matt Markins, Mike Handler, and Chris Marchand, *Resilient: Child Discipleship and the Fearless Future of the Church* (Streamwood, IL: Awana, 2020), 28.

11. "Shine," Newsboys, by Steve Taylor and Peter Furler, track 2 on the album *Going Public*, Star Song, 1994, https://genius.com/Newsboys-shine-lyrics.

12. DC Talk, *Jesus Freak*, ForeFront/Virgin, 1995.

13. Dale Hudson, *If Disney Ran Your Children's Ministry: 10 Keys from Disney's Success* (Kidminhouse, 2016).

14. Justyn Smith, *Kidmin, Trust and Pixie Dust: Unlocking the Magic of Children's Ministry* (Kidmin Magic, 2023).

15. Brett McCracken, "Cool Christianity Is (Still) a Bad Idea," Gospel News Network, August 24, 2020, gospelnewsnetwork.org/2020/08/24/cool-christianity-is-still-a-bad-idea/.

16. Mark Sayers, *Disappearing Church: From Cultural Relevance to Gospel Resilience* (Chicago: Moody Publishers, 2016), 12.

17. David Kinnaman and Mark Matlock, *Faith for Exiles: 5 Ways for a New Generation to Follow Jesus in Digital Babylon* (Grand Rapids, MI: Baker Books, 2019), 32.

18. Christian Smith and Melinda Lundquist Denton, *Soul Searching: The Religious and Spiritual Lives of American Teenagers* (UK: Oxford University Press, 2005).

19. John Mark Comer and Mark Sayers, "What Is Post-Christian Culture?," January 13, 2021, *This Cultural Moment* podcast, https://www.youtube.com/watch?v=yK6EwF3YZAM.

20. Elton Trueblood, *The Predicament of Modern Man* (Elizabethtown, KY: Yokefellow Press), 1944.

21. Gabe Lyons with John Mark Comer, "What's the Future of the Church?," April 8, 2021, *Q Ideas Podcast*, https://qpodcast.libsyn.com/episode-188-whats-the-future-of-the-church-john-mark-comer.

Chapter 4: Charting the New Map

1. Joel Scandrett, "The Road to the Future Runs Through the Past," *Christian History*, 2019, Issue 129, christianhistoryinstitute.org/magazine/article/the-road-to-the-future-runs-through-the-past.

2. Elton John, "Rocket Man," Honky Château, DJM, 1972.

3. If you've not seen the documentary *The Social Dilemma*, about the impact of giving our children technology that we do not fully understand how it is forming them, consider checking it out: https://www.thesocialdilemma.com/.

4. Ed Stetzer, *Christians in the Age of Outrage: How to Bring Our Best When the World Is at Its Worst* (Carol Stream, IL: Tyndale House, 2018).

5. Jim Nicodem, *Bible Savvy Series: Epic* (Chicago: Moody Publishers, 2013), 25.

6. Eugene H. Peterson, *A Long Obedience in the Same Direction: Discipleship in an Instant Society* (Downers Grove, IL: InterVarsity Press, 1980), 11.

7. John Mark Comer, *The Ruthless Elimination of Hurry* (Colorado Springs: WaterBrook, 2019), 77.

8. Jim Davis, Michael Graham and Ryan P. Burge, *The Great Dechurching: Who's Leaving, Why Are They Going, and What Will It Take to Bring Them Back?* (Grand Rapids, MI: Zondervan, 2023), Kindle, 239.

9. Valerie Bell, Matt Markins, and Mike Handler, *Resilient: Child Discipleship and the Fearless Future of the Church* (St. Charles, IL: Awana, 2020), 168.

10. Ibid., 171.

11. Deuteronomy 6:4–9.

12. Christian Smith and Patricia Snell, *Souls in Transition: The Religious and Spiritual Lives of Emerging Adults* (New York: Oxford University Press, 2009), 227. Emphasis in original.

13. Research Project Seven commissioned by Awana, Barna Group, *Children's Ministry in a New Reality: Building Church Communities That Cultivate Lasting Faith* (Ventura, CA: Barna Group, 2022), 77.

14. Center on the Developing Child (2015), *The Science of Resilience* (InBrief), retrieved from www.developingchild.harvard.edu.

15. The Springtide Series on Mental Health, *Mental Health & Gen Z: What Educators Need to Know* (Winona, MN: Springtide Research Institute, 2023), 31.

16. Matt Markins, *The Faith of Our Children: Eight Timely Research Insights for Discipling the Next Generation* (Nashville, TN: Randall House Publishers, 2023), 19.

17. Jon Tyson and Heather Grizzle, *A Creative Minority: Influencing Culture Through Redemptive Participation* (New York: Jon Tyson and Heather Grizzle, 2016), 27.

18. John Mark Comer and Mark Sayers, "The Secular Salvation Schema," January 13, 2021, *This Cultural Moment* podcast, https://www.youtube.com/watch?v=2ngOELRoCLU.

19. Mark 1:14–15, Matthew 5–7.

20. Markins, *The Faith of Our Children*, 31.

21. Comer and Sayers, *This Cultural Moment*.

22. Bell, Markins, and Handler, *Resilient*, chapter 8.

Intermission

1. Fyodor Dostoyevsky, *Demons: A Novel in Three Parts,* trans. Larissa Volokhonsky (London: Vintage, 1994), 38, 718.

Chapter 5: Our Single Most Strategic Opportunity

1. Joel Mathis, "Why U.S. Teens Aren't Getting Their Driver's Licenses," *The Week*, February 16, 2023, theweek.com/travel/1020987/why-us-teens-arent-getting-their-drivers-licenses.

2. Marc Yoder, "Why Youth Leave the Church: 10 Surprising Reasons Teens Disappear," *Church Leaders*, May 22, 2023, www.churchleaders.com/youth/166129-marc-solas-10-surprising-reasons-our-kids-leave-church.html.

3. Aaron Earls, "Who Is the New Church Dropout?," *Lifeway Research*, June 14, 2022, research.lifeway.com/2022/06/13/who-is-the-new-church-dropout/.

4. Statistic about 1 in 3 adults: David Roach, "Church Attendance Dropped Among Young People, Singles, Liberals," *Christianity Today*, January 9, 2023, www.christianitytoday.com/news/2023/january/pandemic-church-attendance-drop-aei-survey-young-people-eva.html.

5. Edgar Allan Poe, *Complete Stories of Edgar Allan Poe* (New York: Doubleday, 1966).

6. "Research Shows That Spiritual Maturity Process Should Start at a Young Age," Barna Group, January 12, 2024, www.barna.com/research/research-shows-that-spiritual-maturity-process-should-start-at-a-young-age/.

7. Ibid.

8. Howard Culbertson, *At What Age Do Americans Become Christian?*, home. snu.edu/~hculbert/ages.htm#:~:text=Another%20survey%20cited%20 by%20the,are%20children%20or%20early%20youth.

9. Research Project Seven commissioned by Awana, Barna Group, *Children's Ministry in a New Reality: Building Church Communities that Cultivate Lasting Faith* (Ventura, CA: Barna Group, 2022), 11.

Chapter 6: Getting Unstuck from Our Stalemate: Moving from Dialogue to Declaration

1. "Stalemate," *Collins English Dictionary*, https://www.collinsdictionary.com/us/dictionary/english/stalemate, accessed February 7, 2024.

2. "Stalemate," *Cambridge Dictionary*, https://dictionary.cambridge.org/us/dictionary/english/stalemate.

3. George Barna, *Transforming Children into Spiritual Champions: Why Children Should Be Your Church's #1 Priority* (Grand Rapids, MI: Baker Books, reprint ed., 2013), 90.

4. George Barna, *Revolutionary Parenting: What the Research Shows Really Works* (Carol Stream, IL: Tyndale; reprint ed., 2010), 76.

5. Research Project Seven commissioned by Awana, Barna Group, *Children's Ministry in a New Reality: Building Church Communities That Cultivate Lasting Faith* (Ventura, CA: Barna Group, 2022).

6. To our knowledge, this may be the only research commissioned on "How Children's Ministry Leaders Spend Their Time" to establish a baseline of the degree to which churches are or are not actually "training" parents on "how" to disciple their children.

7. Barna Group, *Children's Ministry in a New Reality*, 34.

8. Research Project Eight, commissioned by Awana, 5by5 Research Agency (Nashville, TN, 2022), 103.

9. Matt Markins, *The Faith of Our Children: Eight Timely Research Insights for Discipling the Next Generation*, (Nashville, TN: Randall House Publishers, 2023), 70.

10. Ibid., 71.

11. Research Project Eight, 105.

12. Ibid., 129.

13. Ibid., 104.

14. Ibid., 106.

15. Ibid., 112.

Chapter 7: The Formational Church

1. John F. Kennedy, "We Choose to Go to the Moon," September 12, 1962, Rice University, www.rice.edu/jfk-speech.

2. Eugene H. Peterson, *A Long Obedience in the Same Direction: Discipleship in an Instant Society* (Westmont, IL: IVP Books, 1980), Kindle.

3. Jonathan K. Dodson, *Gospel-Centered Discipleship* (Wheaton, IL: Crossway, 2022), 29.

4. William D. Phillips, *The Worlds of Christopher Columbus* (New York: Cambridge University Press, 1993).

5. NASA, "Mars Climate Orbiter Mishap Investigation Board Phase I Report," November 10, 1999.

6. Shaun McKinley, personal post, *Facebook*, October 20, 2023, 9:00 a.m., https://www.facebook.com/story.php/?id=1088932135&story_fbid=10224342499325293&paipv=0&eav=AfYhIv04iQXIEUgLKQQv58S-jggUJHZ4tQ49DD0KFHivznGOx9Dw2PQL-EeoaemPwx88&_rdr.

7. Dietrich Bonhoeffer, *Life Together and Prayerbook of the Bible* (Minneapolis, MN: Fortress Press, 2004), Kindle, 31.

8. Ibid., 47.

9. Philip Slater, *Pursuit of Loneliness* (Boston: Beacon, 1970), 7–8.

10. Yes, we know this point is hotly debated in recent years, with Lebron James the choice of some fans. But for our money, MJ remains the GOAT!

11. Jonathan Edwards, "A Farewell Sermon Preached at the First Precinct in Northampton, After the People's Public Rejection of Their Minister . . . on June 22, 1750," in *Sermons and Discourses, 1743–1758*, The Works of Jonathan Edwards Series, vol. 25, ed. Wilson H. Kimnach (New Haven, CT: Yale University Press, 2006), 25, 484.

12. John Piper, "Let No One Despise You for Your Youth: A Vision for the Next Generation," Desiring God, April 20, 2008, www.desiringgod.org/messages/let-no-one-despise-you-for-your-youth.

Chapter 8: The Formational Home

1. Research Project Eight, commissioned by Awana, 5by5 Research Agency (Nashville, TN, 2022), 114.

2. *Forrest Gump*, directed by Robert Zemeckis, performances by Tom Hanks, Robin Wright, and Gary Sinise, Paramount Pictures, 1994.

3. The Isthmian Games, *Ancient Olympics*, 2012, ancientolympics.arts.kuleuven.be/eng/TB003EN.html.

4. Tedd Tripp, *Shepherding a Child's Heart* (Wapwallopen, PA: Shepherd Press, 1995), 46.

5. Phil and Diane Comer, *Raising Passionate Jesus Followers: The Power of Intentional Parenting* (Grand Rapids, MI: Zondervan, 2018), 79. An amazing practical resource for new and young families that provides a framework and structure for discipleship that works.

6. Daniel A. Cox, "Emerging Trends and Enduring Patterns in American Family Life," *The Survey Center on American Life*, February 9, 2022, www.americansurveycenter.org/research/emerging-trends-and-enduring-patterns-in-american-family-life/#The_Challenge_of_Raising_Children.

7. "American Time Use Survey Summary—2022 A01 Results," U.S. Bureau of Labor Statistics, June 22, 2023, www.bls.gov/news.release/atus.nr0.htm.

8. Greg McKeown, *Essentialism: The Disciplined Pursuit of Less* (London: Penguin UK: Virgin Books, 2021).

9. Albert-László Barabási, *Bursts: the Hidden Pattern Behind Everything We Do* (New York: Penguin: Plume, 2011).

10. Justin Whitmel Earley, *Habits of the Household: Practicing the Story of God in Everyday Family Rhythms* (Grand Rapids, MI: Zondervan, 2021). Earley's book is a great resource for families. It would be a wonderful gift for new parents or parents who are new to your church.

11. John Mark Comer, *The Ruthless Elimination of Hurry: How to Stay Emotionally Healthy and Spiritually Alive in the Chaos of the Modern World* (Colorado Springs: WaterBrook, 2019). Comer's site, https://johnmarkcomer.com, is packed full of discipleship resources for adults that a family can engage in.

12. Jon Tyson, *The Intentional Father: A Practical Guide to Raise Sons of Courage and Character* (Grand Rapids, MI: Baker Books, 2021). Tyson's work also can be accessed through PrimalPath.co.

13. Larry Fowler, *Raising a Modern-Day Joseph: A Timeless Strategy for Growing Great Kids* (Colorado Springs: David C. Cook, 2009).

14. Hillary Rodham Clinton, *It Takes a Village* (New York: Simon & Schuster, 2007).

15. Francesca A. Marino, "Divorce Rate in the U.S.: Geographic Variation, 2021," Family Profile Nov. 26, 2022 (Bowling Green, OH: National Center for Family & Marriage Research), https://doi.org/10.25035/ncfmr/fp-22-26.

16. Bradford Doolittle and Luke Knox, "How Theo Epstein Transformed the Cubs Roster," *ESPN*, www.espn.com/espn/feature/story/_/id/17711479/how-theo-epstein-transformed-cubs-roster, accessed February 7, 2024.

17. Amanda Seitz, "Loneliness Poses Health Risks as Deadly as Smoking, US Surgeon General Says," *PBS*, Public Broadcasting Service, May 2, 2023, www.pbs.org/newshour/health/loneliness-poses-health-risks-as-deadly-as-smoking-u-s-surgeon-general-says.

18. 25 percent of girls reported having made a suicide plan" as shown on page 226.

19. Sherry Turkle, *Alone Together: Why We Expect More from Technology and Less from Each Other* (New York: Basic Books, 2017), 1.

> "YOU SHALL TEACH THEM DILIGENTLY TO YOUR CHILDREN, AND SHALL TALK OF THEM WHEN YOU SIT IN YOUR HOUSE, AND WHEN YOU WALK BY THE WAY, AND WHEN YOU LIE DOWN, AND WHEN YOU RISE."

DEUTERONOMY 6:7 ESV

Your Go-To for All Things
Child Discipleship

 ChildDiscipleship.com

Powered by Awana

You finished reading!

Did this book help you in some way? If so, please consider writing an honest review wherever you purchase your books. Your review gets this book into the hands of more readers and helps us continue to create biblically faithful resources.

Moody Publishers books help fund the training of students for ministry around the world.

The **Moody Bible Institute** is one of the most well-known Christian institutions in the world, training thousands of young people to faithfully serve Christ wherever He calls them. And when you buy and read a book from Moody Publishers, you're helping make that vital ministry training possible.

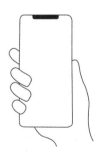

Continue to dive into the Word, *anytime, anywhere.*

Find what you need to take your next step in your walk with Christ: from uplifting music to sound preaching, our programs are designed to help you right when you need it.

Download the **Moody Radio App** and start listening today!

 MOODY Publishers

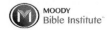 MOODY Bible Institute

 MOODY Radio